HEALTHIER PROFITS

the GREEN FACTOR

Edited by Steve Robinson

Introduction by David Bellamy

with contributions from

John Elkington
Marek Mayer
Timothy O'Riordan
Richard Sandbrook et al
Andrew Warren

Sponsored by

THE ENVIRONMENT FOUNDATION

Promoted by

The Conservation Foundation

The Commonwealth Institute

DESIGN Nick Newbery

TYPESET AND PRINTED BY: Knight & Forster
129 Water Lane
Leeds   LS11 9UB

CONTENTS

SPONSOR'S MESSAGE

What do we mean by healthier profits? Is it or is it not a contradiction in terms? I propose to spin a tale, a fantasy which may perhaps illustrate the theme that there is money in good environmental practices. The story goes like this.

On the west side of our island there is a fertile farming valley where grain grows and cattle wax fat. The valley is watered by a river whose silver links have their birth in the mountains at the head of the vale and fall some 30 miles to a fine estuary. The farmers own the river which years ago supported a large run of salmon and seatrout as well as a teeming population of indigenous fish, insects and river-side animals.

In those far off days anglers came from all over the world to stay in the hotels and farmhouses of the valley to enjoy their sport in the beautiful and productive river. They brought with them employment and additional prosperity. Sadly, however, following two dislocating world wars the farmers were exhorted and pressurised to produce more and more food from the lush acreages beside the river, and in addition, to increase that acreage by draining the riparian marshes. Massive and subsidised loads of nitrogenous fertilisers were poured on to the land to increase its yield. Much of this fertiliser was washed into the gleaming river and promoted the growth of a stifling slime which covered the once shining stones of the river bed. Silage was made on the farms and farmers ignorant of its effect allowed effluent to pollute the feeder streams. Slurries were washed in ever increasing quantities in to the river which gradually but surely began to lose its sparkle as its oxygen content became steadily reduced. The fish population deprived of the teeming insect life began to decline drastically and finally after many years disappeared almost completely. The once shining river became lifeless, a muddy and defiled water course. No fishermen came to the valley now. The netsmen in the estuary were put out of work. The

1

hotels shut down as did many shops in the little town. Fishing rents became a thing of the past. Farming economics then began to change. Sudsidies on fertilisers and on drainage disappeared and quotas on farm products were imposed. Farming incomes dropped and farmers desperately began to look for other ways of utilizing their assets. The river was no longer a resource but could it yet become one in an age when leisure activities were at a premium!

Enormous efforts were made to clean up the river and reoxygenate its flows. Over years this succeeded as environmentally considerate farming and proper management of effluent and slurries became the norm. The river sparkled once more; the salmon and seatrout began to run and breed in ever increasing abundance. Fishermen from all over the world flocked back to the river banks prepared to pay large sums of money, often in valuable foreign currencies, to fish once more. The return of the fishermen to the valley brought employment and an increase in all sorts of economic activity in hotels, shops, petrol stations and the farms themselves. The rents from the river multiplied and the capital value of the river resource increased the value of the farms with riparian rights exceedingly.

That is my fantasy. I hope it illustrates the theme of this book which I am happy that the Environment Foundation is sponsoring.

A word about the Environment Foundation. It is a small charity with limited funds originating from the insurance market. It specialises in encouraging and publicising good Environmental practice and management by a process of leverage using our small funds as a fulcrum to promote research projects, a Pollution Abatement Award and last but not least, this intensely interesting book.

Michael Martin
Chairman
The Environment Foundation

INTRODUCTION

BY DAVID BELLAMY

TECHNOLOGY is the process by which people have conquered the natural world, taming wilderness, turning profit for themselves with no regard to the environment.

Symbiosis is the process by which nature couples the activity of different species to the mutual benefit (profit) of both.

The wages of the former are a divided world, the haves and the have nots of human society both dependent on the life support systems of a world which is now smashed almost beyond repair.

The wages of the latter are the self sufficient, recyling productive living systems which have fed people and their technology and will continue to do so if given a chance.

Conservation is the global voice of concern which warns of impending environmental and hence economic catastrophe.

Symbiotic technology links the two, technology and environment, to the mutual benefit of the natural and people made world.

Conservation though the buzz world of the 80's has been around for a long time supported by some important names and strident voices. Why then hasn't it worked? Why, because it is all too often regarded as being negative, a movement which is always trying to turn the clock back, to stop development and hence profit. The whiplash has therefore been (especially amongst the successful business community who have the "clout" and the money to spearhead change), that conservation is anti

3

people, anti jobs, anti progress, anti everything. They have the money, the power and the know how to publicise their point of view and cover up any horrors their action perpetrates en route.

There are two methods to combat this, the one to beat them, the other to join them.

The first is based on laws both local and international and on pacts and agreements. Laws which have to be enforced and agreements which have to be kept. All this, though of key importance, costs money, takes time and is in the interim, before complete acceptance, looked upon as another negative aspect of conservation.

The join them way is, as I and the book believe, the way ahead. It shows how technology (not benign, luddite back to nature stuff, but aggressive, innovative job and wealth creating technology) can work within and not against the environment to the mutual benefit of all who are dependent on the life support systems of planet earth.

The world of thinking people abhor what they see around them — expanding desert, aggro-farming, soil erosion, pollution, destruction of the landscapes, extinction of plants and animals, decimation of their heritage. They are asking what future is there for our children. The first company who proudly goes the way of symbiotic technology, showing their workforce and management the day to day benefits in their own and the wider environment, showing the shareholders the way to long term profits, but above all using it in their advertising and public image, will become the brand leaders not only of the products but of the new way of corporate life.

Read this book and move with your company towards healthier profits and hence healthier living.

The Conservation Foundation

4

CHAPTER 1

THE
FATAL
ERROR

LIFE OR DEATH, profit or loss, success or disaster; often the fatal error is not considering the environmental factor. This books cuts through the confusing jungle of moral-sounding arguments around environmental issues to show the practical reasons why it is in the decision maker's interests to consider the environmental factor. It will show there's commercial sense in satisfying human needs with environmentally friendlier technologies and that these are already appearing through normal business and social pressures.

One such pressure is self interest, a major motivating force far stronger than any legislation. After all, though people may cooperate with laws as it is in their interest not to go to jail, people still break laws out of self interest. Short term self interest, then, besides being a prime reason cited for polluting, is an important reason for considering the environmental factor. Try this test: Do you know anyone that has insulated their roof? Why did they do it? Was it to conserve global energy reserves or to save money? Most likely to save money. And companies supplied the insulation to make money, not because they were concerned about thermal pollution. Conservation happens to be a by-product of the transaction. So **short term self interest can be one of the most powerful forces working for conservation.**

A lesson from History

Considering the environmental factor is important. And many

historical examples of the adverse affects on decision makers' interests of poor environmental awareness and management illustrate the point. Just how many communities or even civilizations have collapsed through abusing their supporting ecosystems or eroding their resource base may never be known but these cultures would have had organisations or hierarchies and these would have contained decision makers. It follows that the interests of these decision makers in administration, commerce, militarism or religion would all have been adversely affected through their failing to adequately manage interactions with the local environment (SEE BOX 1).

Yet we're often led to believe that messing up the environment is a modern phenomenon. This particular set of post industrial revolution generations is accused of tossing environmental common sense out the window. There seems to be a myth that previous generations lived in idyllic harmony with the natural world and consequently they would hold up their hands in horror if they knew what was happening now.

Did the decision makers in lost cultures ignore environmental advice? Certainly the advice, though not of the quality of that now available, would have been there. Roman agricultural manuals outline the need for good husbandry and Plato talked of the bones of the earth showing through due to human activity. If advice was ignored it could have been for similar reasons to those currently causing environmental guidance to fall on apparently deaf ears.

Human nature dictates that in the vanished cultures there would have been the pessimists and doom-mongers amongst the advisors whose dire predictions undermined the value of more credible advice. More recently, the industrial revolution gave modern doom-mongers something to get their teeth into. The introduction of the train, for instance, produced a rash of predictions, perhaps the quaintest being that passengers would asphyxiate at high speed!

Even carefully and responsibly making predictions from current trends is a hazardous business. Stanley Jevons was one of the foremost economists of his day and in 1865 he theorised that the rising cost of coal due to increasing demand would check the growth of prosperity in Victorian Britain. He did not consider petroleum would ever be a significant fuel. His forecasts were made on the basis of the best information available to him at the time. That he was a little off target demonstrates the problems of trying to produce a picture of the future. Probably the most accurate definition of the hit and miss nature of forecasting comes from business where it's been likened to driving a car blindfold to the directions of someone sitting in the back seat looking out the rear window.

BOX 1

Political Power BC Salted Away

In the 18th Century BC political power shifted away from the southern cities of Sumer. It's thought the shift took place because cereal growing conditions in the more northerly districts of Lower Mesopotamia did not deteriorate so badly through environmental mismanagement.

In the third millennium BC the earliest known major canal in the area had been constructed to lead water from the Tigris to a disputed area between two settlements which had previously been supplied with water from the Euphrates. The fate of the 'new' canal and its associated schemes is well documented and, though it made more water available and could have extended cultivated areas, large scale irrigation schemes in the southern parts of Lower Mesopotamia were not successful in the long term.

Temple records from the time seem to show salination of the fields appearing, then its spread to more and more land. Salination occurs when the water table rises close to the surface; water evaporates leaving behind the minerals and salts it contained. In this case the water table rose through over irrigation and neglect of drainage as gradients in the area are negligible.

The gradual salination is probably the reason why the records show an alteration in the proportions of wheat and barley harvested. Around 3,500 BC the two cereals were equally important but by 2,400 BC barley, more tolerant of salt conditions, had risen to 84% of the recorded harvest. By 2,100 BC it comprised 98% of recorded harvest and around 1,700 BC no wheat at all appears to have been harvested. The increasing proportion of barley harvested was accompanied though by continually declining yields.

Cultivation shifted towards the north-west, and land was abandoned on a wide scale as the state, through declining authority, could not cope with the pressures for change.

But all is not well . . .

The problem is that many of the more recent predictions on the environment seem uncomfortably close to coming true. Most are based on direct and irrefutable observed fact: once abundant species have disappeared and fertile areas have turned to desert. Something can plainly be seen to be wrong.

There are those in key positions who do not seem able or willing to see this and, as if by way of compensation to the doom-mongers, there have been and still are those with complacently held and grossly wrong views on environmental issues. Radiation was thought not to be too bad for you, nor was smog and both cocaine and heroin were initially regarded as safe preparations. Smoking was positively beneficial for all kinds of reasons.

But issues like the effects of radiation, Thalidomide or exposure to asbestos fibres have shaken public confidence in the "official" view. The sceptics and dissenters of the 50's and 60's have developed into the sophisticated action groups and lobbyists comprising the contemporary environmental movement. Now the message preached loud and long by various groups in recent times is that the global environment is in deep trouble.

The issues concerning environmentalists are well documented. They are linked to the sheer scale of human activity as well as the increased capabilities brought by modern technology. Human numbers have increased to nearly five billion and this puts unprecedented pressure on the systems and resource base that support our activities. In parts of the world these pressures have locked people into a miserable cycle of environmental and economic poverty (SEE BOX 2).

Yet some still seem to regard the earth as having inexhaustible resources to provide for our needs. It is so big they feel it has infinite capacity to absorb what they throw away, even if the waste is toxic. Valuable cropland is sealed under paved roads, cities and other developments and soil is washed or blown away, lost through poor agricultural practice. Deforestation and overgrazing lead to the spread of deserts.

The forests have been and are being logged at an alarming rate though the long term consequences are unknown. The short term consequences unfortunately are all too evident as flash flooding, sedimentation and water shortages radically affect food production in some critical areas. In fact the tropical forests are almost a huge confidence trick, their superb biological efficiency disguising the paucity

BOX 2

CYCLE OF DESPAIR: ENVIRONMENTAL & ECONOMIC POVERTY IN THE THIRD WORLD

Economic Crisis

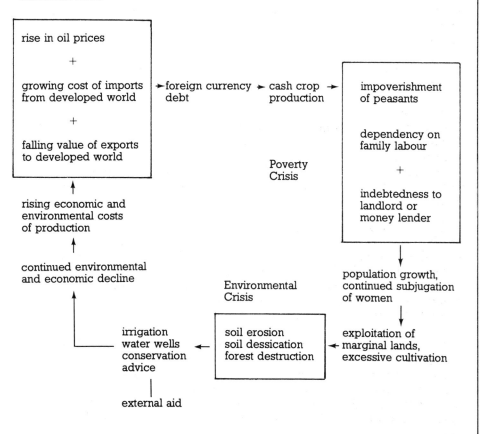

rise in oil prices

+

growing cost of imports from developed world

+

falling value of exports to developed world

↑

rising economic and environmental costs of production

↑

continued environmental and economic decline

→foreign currency debt ➤ cash crop production →

Poverty Crisis

impoverishment of peasants

dependency on family labour

+

indebtedness to landlord or money lender

population growth, continued subjugation of women

Environmental Crisis

soil erosion
soil dessication
forest destruction

exploitation of marginal lands, excessive cultivation

irrigation
water wells
conservation
advice

external aid

The three "crises" of the third world are indebtedness, poverty and environmental destruction. Each tragically reinforces the other.

of their supporting soils. The goods and services they provide or could provide like building materials, fuel and drugs have been lost forever at the price of relatively little immediate gain.

Fisheries are ruthlessly overfished though the techniques exist to manage them correctly. Tons of by-catch are taken and simply thrown away in fishing for certain high value species like prawns. Inland fisheries are polluted and lost, water courses contaminated and inshore fishing grounds threatened or lost through sedimentation, pollution or dumping.

The Irish potato famine of the 1840s where potato blight led to death by starvation of 2 million showed how vulnerable a population depending on one crop is. Yet now just a handful of mega-crops are relied on to provide the bulk of the global food supply. The product of the Green Revolution which started in the 1940s, these crops heavily depend on chemical fertilisers and pesticides for the vitally necessary high yields. Some of these chemicals have proved dangerously persistent. Some have destroyed the enemies of pests and the pollinators of crops.

The mega-crops are planted crowded together in hectares of dense monocultures which are vulnerable to attack by pests and disease. The plant breeders and geneticists have to work to keep one jump ahead of rapidly mutating crop pathogens which would race through the fields like fire. The trouble is they are increasingly restricted in the material they have to work with as natural strains and varieties are lost and older "inefficient" breeds are allowed to die out.

Despite its drawbacks, the Green Revolution has bought the time needed to sort out some of the long term solutions to these global problems. One major set of answers is in the World Conservation Strategy which was launched in 1980 defining three main objectives: to maintain life support systems, preserve genetic diversity and ensure we utilize species and ecosystems like fisheries and forests sustainably. It was aimed at decision makers and the document encouraged countries to prepare their own national conservation strategies. It also maintained that conservation and development are inextricably linked. Conservation cannot succeed without sustainable development and development will not succeed unless conservation issues are considered.

Discounting environmental advice

Now that some of the answers to environmental problems have been or are on the way to being formulated the trouble is that not enough notice appears to be taken of them. In fact it is possible to speculate on reasons why many decision makers are slow in appreciating that environmental factors **can** affect their activities. Maybe some decision makers feel the doom-mongers have cried wolf too often. Many could be put off entertaining any of the proposed solutions by bogey-words like "conservation" which outside of energy conservation seems synonymous with hostile pressure groups and tough legislation. Others may think the issues they are concerned about are too remote and will not affect them (SEE BOX 3).

BOX 3

Managerial Commonsense....

There are three rules so fundamental to corporate survival and success that they are rarely quoted:

1. Generate revenue

2. Keep options open

3. Maintain production

or (turn the page)

Conservation Claptrap?

The World Conservation Strategy (WCS) was launched in 1980 and is based on these very three basic principles.

1. Just as the company needs to generate revenue and maintain its life-support, cash, the WCS aims to maintain essential ecological processes and so protect life-support systems.

2. Whether in research, location, staffing, sales or production methods the company with the best chances of success is the one that stays flexible and keeps its options open. The WCS aims to keep options open by preserving genetic diversity for the security of food supplies and the industries that use living resources.

3. Maintaining production of goods or services is a fundamental prerequisite of corporate survival let alone success. The WCS aims to ensure the natural production of species and ecosystems (like fisheries, forests and grazing lands) is used sustainably so it can continue to support rural communities and dependent industries.

Considering each possibility in turn, the crying wolf argument pursued to extremes simply results in tit for tat exchanges of "You were wrong about . . .". Two or more wrongs do not cancel each other out or make an environmental right. Being wrong on one issue does not necessarily mean being incorrect on the next one. It just undermines other peoples' faith in the opinions expressed. Yet sound practical advice on environmental issues is available.

Secondly conservation has to be a bogey-word. Surely it has such a panoply of meanings and so many adverse associations in the mind of decision makers that no self respecting PR agency would recommend using the word if starting a campaign from scratch? Yet there are attempts to sell conservation to decision makers as something of direct benefit to them at the same time as their activities are openly criticized or interfered with by pressure groups who use the word in a different context or who even have it as part of their name. Using the word "conservation" in so many key statements must alienate some decision makers and so prevent them from heeding environmental advice on matters which could directly affect their interests.

Some decision makers may simply think of environmental groups as a uniform body often hostile to many of their activities because of their actions, policies and, indeed, their association with the word "conservation". An industry homily encapsulates this view: "Environmentalists! Let 'em starve and freeze in the dark!".

Though talked of as "the other side", the environmental lobby is best seen as a loose, sometimes uneasy, federation of groups gathered under a banner that's common mainly in name only. They may have to compete for funds from the same limited sources. Different groups can have conflicting aims, say where a residents' association pushes for an alternative proposed motorway route away from its own area but through a wood or feature of interest to another group.

The active members of these organisations are highly committed people, prepared to risk both life and liberty to draw attention to particular injustices, environmental hazards and their point of view. The limpet mining and sinking of Greenpeace's flagship **Rainbow Warrior** in Auckland before she sailed to protest about French nuclear testing in the Pacific indicated how far confrontational conservation can escalate. Yet despite this dramatic illustration of the risks they face, people will always get involved in causes they feel strongly about.

Confrontation conservation never was popular in the business community. And now, correctly or not, there are cases where it is perceived as a luxury to be afforded by people in full employment or in an area unaffected by the particular problem. In part the problem lies in

THE **RAINBOW WARRIOR**, SUNK BY LIMPET MINES IN AUCKLAND: WILL
CONFRONTATION ONLY PRODUCE MORE DEDICATED PEOPLE TO
CONFRONT?
(photo: Greenpeace)

peoples' preconceptions, stirred when the word "conservation" enters an argument. This happened on the Scottish island of Islay when conservationists wanting to preserve a winter habitat for rare geese clashed with locals who had been led to believe the jobs from a local whisky distillery's plans for the area were at risk. Farmers on the island remained unsympathetic to both the geese and the conservationists' case claiming that the birds consumed vast quantities of grass which could feed more animals. Despite the protestations of the environmentalists to the contrary, locals would only see conservation as a force standing in the way of their own interests.

The existence or possibility of environmental legislation could act as a disincentive to decision makers to think further about the environmental factor beyond mere compliance. In turn environmentalists have to face the accusation that they place too much faith in legislation and, apart from alienating industrialists, this faith could create other problems for their case. For instance, new laws on the environment need cooperative legislators. The possibility of crying wolf becomes another hazard when trying to prod legislators into action. In a theoretical (and unlikely) case, **if** a virus rather than Acid Rain turned out to be principally responsible for killing the trees in European forests, the laissez faire attitude of any government doing little on power station and motor emissions control would be reinforced; a step backwards if presenting proposals for legislation on other contentious issues like disposing of radioactive waste.

Legislation though creates new market conditions. Whilst all this prevarication and delay goes on, new recovery or control equipment industries are denied markets. The prizes, profits and jobs, may go to other countries with more advanced controls whose new industries are in a position to export if and when the legislation is enacted in the prevaricating country.

Legislation and agreements are vitally necessary in certain circumstances, say on health and safety or restricting trade in rare species, but can't be a universal environmental panacea. Tough laws will not work in parts of the world where enforcement is lax or non-existent; no one would be too interested in applying stringent emissions controls in a war zone. So even when legislation can be enacted with some hope of effect it cannot be relied upon for total environmental protection. Some crimes like robbery and murder have been legislated against in all probability since the beginnings of organised society but they're still being committed.

The role of greener legislation is best illustrated by considering one of the first lessons of management: learning how to motivate people.

Discovering the disincentives is just as important as finding out the incentives. Rules and regulations can be a disincentive. It is possible to coerce colleagues and staff but their productivity will be much less than if they had approached a particular task willingly. The rules of the workplace are there as guides for the protection of staff, customers and the organisation itself and to be effective people have to respect and follow those rules. The situation in the global workplace is no different. Legislation should be regarded and developed as a framework within which commonsense, commercial acumen and compassion can be applied.

Respecting the need for some environmental controls may be difficult for some decision makers. It means understanding what the World Conservation Strategy was driving at linking conservation and development. Superficially this does seem to contain a massive contradiction. People need food, fuel and water and to earn the means to pay for them in factories, offices and shops. A certain standard of living is expected in many parts of the world. At the same time some want to see aspects of their surroundings preserved, where they do not conflict with immediate plans. However, the link between these two apparent irreconcilables is that successful development often **has** to take account of conservation factors, as the final chapter of this book aims to show.

The final reason some decision makers may not take too much notice of the proposed answers to environmental problems is that the issues themselves seem remote and irrelevant. Unfortunately this isn't the case. The effects and the lessons are there but are swiftly forgotten. The 70s oil price hikes should have hammered home that some resources are finite, the collapse of one fishery after another that renewable resources need careful management. Disaster whether it's famine or financial collapse is not hard to notice. But the reasons have not been fully understood though they're not hard to see either. The environmentalists' claim is that taking account of conservation issues at the planning stage can help avert some of these crises.

The trouble is this hasn't been said in a way that appeals to decision makers. If it had, more would be considering the environmental factor at the planning stage. The conservationists have achieved some spectacular successes but these have mainly been linked to individual issues from saving whales to having lead removed from petroleum. Yet saving species or individual habitats are really the Dunkirks of the environmental movement. The conservation groups are great tacticians and powerful lobbyists as oil companies, chemical giants, the nuclear industry and many others have discovered. But the message that considering the environmental factor pays still needs getting through to

16

the majority of those holding key positions. No one, though, feels inclined to listen to someone who they feel is threatening disruption if they don't agree.

But the fatal error a decision maker can make is failing to take account of environmental issues in plans and developments. Yet acting to avoid catastrophe whether this is loss of food, markets, profits, jobs or votes is a prime function of decision makers. If key people in collapsed and lost cultures had had their way their civilizations would have persisted but they didn't despite their decision makers acting out of self interest often presumably on the basis of the best information available to them at the time.

Better environmental information and advice is now available. Also the home insulation case quoted earlier is not unique for there are many emerging environmentally friendlier techniques which decision makers should be researching, developing and adopting out of their own short term self interest. These methods, which in effect conserve and develop, still satisfy the needs of individuals, decision makers and organisations and can lead to healthier profits in both the balance sheet **and** environmental senses. But before looking at their appearance in various sectors it is necessary to define what these techniques are and say how they can be found — and that's what the next chapter is all about.

CHAPTER 2

THE SIGNPOST TO SUCCESS

MAGINE TRYING TO GET TO GRIPS with subjects like computer programming, natural selection or nuclear physics if they didn't actually have names or anything else to refer to them by. This problem is probably the major stumbling block to decision makers appreciating the importance of considering the environmental factor for there does not appear to be a name for the environmentally friendly techniques that satisfy human needs. If these were named it would help decision makers understand their nature and comprehend the impact such activities can have on their interests. They could then develop appropriate policies toward them.

Consider the lack of a name problem from the point of view of having to write this book: how can it go on and consider a whole range of activities that do not have a collective name? How can readers be expected to understand the arguments in favour of researching, developing and adopting the nameless something? To fully appreciate their significance the decision maker would have to be able to classify any examples cited under one clearly defined umbrella term denoting environmentally friendlier technologies that satisfy human needs (SEE BOX 1).

Admittedly it is possible to get by without knowing the formal terminology and thinking connected to a subject: some business lecturers ruefully acknowledge that many gifted entrepreneurs unconsciously

BOX 1

The Box With No Name

Calls for environmentally friendlier technologies are nothing new . . .

In 1968 silted dams, polluted irrigation schemes, ruined fisheries and horrendous health problems were amongst the cases presented at a conference on international development and ecology. Held at Washington University the conference examined instances where often vastly expensive schemes had run into difficulties because the environmental factor had not been considered at the planning stage.

Summarising the conference in its accompanying book, **"The Careless Technology"** Barry Commoner said "What is called for, I believe, is a new technology, designed to meet the needs of the human condition and of the natural environment . . ."

Well the new technology is here, having appeared mainly through normal commercial forces. And those exploiting it are doing rather well. Trouble is until it is named how will the rest of us know what to look for . . .?

apply sophisticated managerial tools. After all, most are common sense. But, by naming approaches like management by objectives and formalising their structure it is possible to teach others so they can benefit from using them. Naming processes generally helps people identify and fully exploit the opportunities they offer. This is how knowledge, ideas and concepts are spread. Terminology helps advance a subject for, though domestic animal breeds were improved in the 18th century through artificial selection, publishing theories under the terms "inheritance" and "genetics" have led to further gains from genetic engineering in medicine and agriculture.

There are some terms about connected with the sector we're considering like "alternative", "appropriate" and "intermediate" technology but these are not exactly what's wanted.

Appropriate technology primarily refers to new rural-based technologies in the Third World which are suited to or necessary under specific human circumstances. This, therefore, may be using bicycle power in husking corn but it can also mean applying DDT powder by hand to a much needed subsistence crop. In other words, "appropriate" methods may be appropriate to immediate circumstances and need not necessarily be kinder to the environment. Alternative technology implies the need for developing radically different products and processes to contemporary conventional ones but many environmentally friendly techniques, like insulating the loft, don't really fall in this category. Intermediate technology actually forms a group within the nameless category being considered. It cannot be elevated to the status of an umbrella term as it would not cover sophisticated developments, like pollution control equipment, that are environmentally friendlier.

So before going any further **a simple term is needed describing all environmentally kinder processes satisfying human needs.**

Naming what to look for

Deriving a term is remarkably straightforward. It needs two basic components: one should define human activities and the other should describe people's relationship with the environment when benefiting through these activities.

First is considering a word describing any human activity. To show why human activity is special it has to be contrasted with the natural world. Here animals and plants can be seen essentially as living tool kits, fitted out with all the accessories necessary for surviving in a particular ecological niche. Humans, though, are woefully short on adaptations like beaks, trunks, or webbed feet. There's only a large brain on top of a clumsy upright stance prone to back trouble.

The upshot of this is that any human survival equipment has to be adapted, adopted or made. As this happens somewhere in every chain of human activity, human actions can be classed as "technologies" for the purposes of deriving the new term.

Admittedly there are some notable animal tool users: sea otters may float on their backs hammering tasty clams open on a flat rock anvil balanced on their chest, certain birds use cactus spines to winkle grubs out of bark and chimpanzees have been known to seize sticks as weapons. But no one could seriously refer to animal tool users as technologists.

So, in the term being developed to describe environmentally kinder techniques satisfying human needs, the word describing any human activities must be **technology.**

Now to qualify the types of technology being considered and describe people's relationship with the environment when benefiting from using these. What is needed is a word that actually illustrates these technologies hold an advantage for the user alongside being kinder to the environment. After all, if there is no immediate benefit to the user, why bother with the environmentally more acceptable method? This means a word describing mutually advantageous associations benefiting widely different parties at the same time is required. In this case, the parties couldn't be more different being people and the environment.

Symbiosis, a term borrowed from biology, provides the answer. Strictly it means living together, though now it is popularly applied to situations where unlikely partners both benefit from their association.

Odd couples living in symbiotic relationships abound in both plant and animal kingdoms. Ant trees, for instance, provide shelter for colonies of ants in specially modified stems and thorns. They also grow food for the ants in sacs or other bodies on stem leaves of flowers. In return the ants protect their tree from herbivores and competing neighbouring plants. One particularly pugnacious species tackles leaf-eating monkeys and even elephants!

There is every possible combination with animal and animal, animal and plant, plant and plant or either plant or animal and bacteria all being found living together. Some examples are quite familiar: lichens are actually a fungus and alga partnership and coral-reef building animals or polyps have resident algae in certain cells. Herbivores like rabbits and cattle don't produce the enzymes for digesting the plant cellulose forming a large part of their diets. The work is done by flourishing gut populations of micro-flora and fauna.

In a wider context, the close relationship between Japanese government and business has been described as Symbiotic and science fiction devotees discovered that the Time Lord, Dr Who of the BBC science fiction series of that name, has a symbiotic relationship with his time machine.

Symbiotic relationships are characterised by the mutual dependence or even inseparability of the partners. Termites are a graphic example of this for the cellulose in their wood diet is digested by one-celled animals called protozoans living in the gut. Heating termites up to a temperature that they can tolerate but which kills the canteen staff ensures tragedy. Despite continuing to consume lots of wood the termites die of starvation. The protozoans aren't around to do the digesting.

So to wrap up defining the new term, look at the fundamental relationship between us and the environment: the human race is dependent on the environment for food and raw materials and the environment now largely depends on humanity for its continued protection. Environmentalists have long argued that if we look after the environment, it can take care of us. So if technology is the word describing the processes of human culture, the term we can use for activities satisfying our needs yet caring for the environment must be **Symbiotic Technology** (or ST for short).

Does it exist?

Now anyone can invent fancy words but who will develop Symbiotic Technologies? The answer is lots of people and many already have. ST exists, produced by normal commercial and social forces for one of the main reasons behind all human activity: satisfying needs. Conservation is often just a by-product. Energy conservation technology is perhaps the most familiar contemporary example though certain types of biotechnology, earthworm technology where farm wastes are broken down by controlled vermicultures, alternative energy supply systems, waste recovery and low waste manufacturing techniques are all Symbiotic Technologies.

New techniques successfully supplant older practices when they appear more attractive for reasons of cost, convenience or even fashion. Like other technologies, ST appears through normal human development. It is adopted because it is more attractive to users and suppliers than conventional options, if they exist. As in the example in the test in Chapter 1, people insulate the roof because the fuel savings seem attractive. Others supply the insulation because it is an attractive commercial proposition. Concern about global energy reserves is rarely voiced by or relevant to the parties in such a transaction.

Often it's concern about costs, efficiency or marketability that fuel the search for more effective techniques rather than worries about the harmful side effects of a conventional technology. Many alternatives found have ST aspects or can be classed as ST. Low temperature detergents, some asbestos-free roofing sheets and low-volume agrochemical applicators where charged droplets "stick" to crop plants all show ST aspects.

Symbiotic Technologies are developed and adopted, **not** primarily out of concern for the environment, but because it makes sound commercial sense. Symbiotic organisms do not live together for the long term benefit of their species, they do so out of short term expediency that happens to benefit the species in the long run. Similarly we do things because short term or relatively short term there's "something-in-it-for-us". Often the side effects of human activites are polluting but if an ST opportunity is found and developed then conservation is the by-product.

Calling the something in something-in-it-for-us "gain" shows how it is the fundamental force motivating behind widely different activities in widely different groups. Subsistence farmers or artisanal fishermen hope immediate survival at the very least is the gain resulting from their efforts for in many poorer countries the difference between success and failure is the difference between life and death. If crops fail or catches are poor the long term advantages to keeping the seed corn or leaving brood or young fish are traded for the gain of immediate survival and they are consumed. You'd do the same in similar circumstances.

Gains for commerce, industry or agrobusiness include profit, growth, improved image or simply commercial survival whereas for governments gain usually boils down to retaining power. Environmental groups gain principally through seeing greater care taken of the environment and act to raise awareness of the need for this care. Individuals look for a variety of gains which after personal survival can be material or aesthetic and include personal security, a family, satisfaction in leisure interests or religion, career goals, material possessions, power, and so on.

Unresolved differences between business and the green lobby are in part attributable to or aggravated by each group's unwillingness to acknowledge or adopt the other's objectives. However, ST acts as a sort of common denominator, for the same means provide the different gains of objectives required by apparently irreconcilable groups. A new development in horticulture demonstrates this: certain growers can gain from cost effective agrobiological sprays, where specially bred pathogens rather than chemicals are targeted cheaply on specific pests. The manufacturers gain from supplying such a product and consumers gain from buying safer produce at similar or lower prices. Government gains from being neatly levered off the horns of an apparent dilemma: conserve (ban chemicals) or develop (allow the best production methods). At the same time the environmentalists gain from seeing greater care taken of the environment through reduced pesticide pollution (SEE BOX 2).

It's possible to confirm ST acts as a common denominator by examining the activities of the three very broad camps involved in the green debate: industry, government and environmentalists. Each in itself is a significant, even powerful group. Now if a Symbiotic Technology offers appropriate gains to a specific group it is likely it would be found being promoted by that particular lobby to further its own ends. That lobby would do so with a high expectation of success as the other groups would be likely to adopt or promote the Symbiotic Technology because of gains it offered them.

This is exactly what happens and that old chestnut energy conservation technology is the best example. A whole new industry has grown up around developing, supplying and installing energy saving and low energy systems because there is a substantial market to support it. Companies, organisations and individuals are interested in saving energy as they want to save money. At the same time energy conservation technology has been promoted by governments and environmental groups because it helps them achieve their own objectives. Government sees reduced energy imports and a more efficient industry able to pay taxes and retain jobs. Environmentalists see greater care taken of the environment through reduced thermal and other pollution and stabilising demand on conventional energy resources.

Some environmentalists may be interested in the possibilities offered by wind power as this cleaner energy source could reduce demand on conventional more polluting sources. Governments may express an interest in wind energy either directly through putting funds into the research efforts as has happened in the U.K. or indirectly, say through tax concessions to those investing in wind turbines as in the U.S. Companies have become involved in the development efforts as potentially the rewards for success are high.

The need to reduce waste through better design is something industry and environmental groups are agreed upon. Value engineering, developing more efficient manufacturing methods, is carried out because it is a vital function if an industry is to remain competitive.

BOX 2

Which Would You Back?

Produced by bio-engineering certain pathogens to target on specific crop pests, Agrobiological pesticides are an excellent example of a Symbiotic Technology as they are cheaper and safer than chemical alternatives and are attractive to growers, innovators, investors, environmentalists and consumers.

PRODUCT DEVELOPMENT	AGROCHEMICALS	AGROBIOLOGICALS
R & D costs	£12 million	£400,000
New products discovery	Screen 15,000 compounds, discover afterwards what targets they control	Target selected on market need; microbial control agents often easy to find
Market size required for profit	£30 million per year to recoup investment: limited to major crops	Markets under £600,000 can be profitable due to low development cost

PRODUCT USE		
Kill	Often 100%	Usually 90–95%
Speed	Usually rapid	Can be slow
Spectrum	Generally broad	Generally narrow
Resistance	Often develops	None yet shown, but microbes also adaptable

PRODUCT SAFETY		
Toxicological testing	Lengthy and costly – £3 million	£40,000
Environmental hazard	Many well known examples	None yet shown
Residues	Interval to harvest usually required	Crop may be harvested immediately

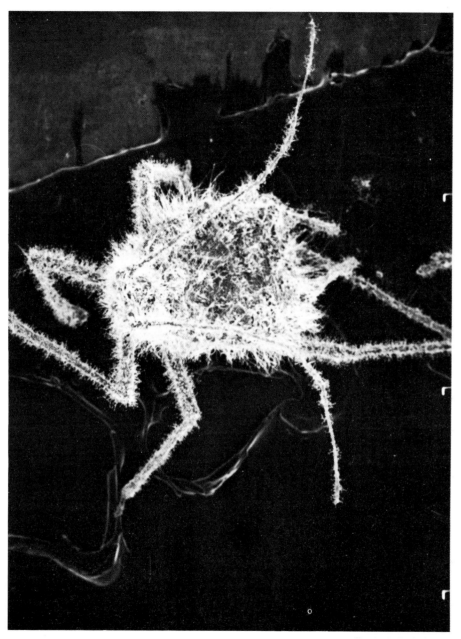

SAFER PEST CONTROL: AN APHID INFECTED WITH THE FUNGUS
VERTICILLIUM LECANII, SPORES OF WHICH ARE CONTAINED IN ONE OF
THE NEW COMMERCIALLY AVAILABLE AGROBIOLOGICAL SPRAYS.
(photo: Microbial Resources)

Environmentalists encourage the activity as they gain through knowing better use is being made of existing resources.

A particular lobby may hop ahead of the others if it realises a technique may ultimately be of interest to groups or individuals, as opposed to the whole, in the one of the other lobbies. For instance one established conservation campaign tactic is pointing out or promoting environmentally kinder substitutes, in effect Symbiotic Technologies, for sensitive products or methods. The vested interests in the controversial methods may ignore the alternative suggestions but there may be other businesses who seize the opportunity. The anti-whaling campaign is one example of this in operation and it's a tactic industry can expect to see more of in the future.

In industry, hopping ahead can mean publicity campaigns based on and exploiting the ecological or implied ecological superiority of a product. There's quite a long list including low temperature detergents, water based coach paints and asbestos-free roofing and insulation materials.

But some companies and innovators may go for Symbiotic Technologies simply because of the greater short term gain they offer over alternatives, not because they acknowledge their ecological superiority. This is evident for, just as the harmful side effects of some new products were not fully appreciated at the time of introduction, it follows there are those where conservation remains unadvertised as a by-product because it has not been recognised or is thought irrelevant to the central thrust of a marketing effort. One such case is home carbonating kits, where fizzy drinks can be made domestically using concentrate, water and an attractively styled carbonating unit. These offer the consumer cheaper soft drinks and fun for the kids but it is not widely advertised that the kits cut down the need for bottles and even fuel for transport: only the concentrate is moved as the bulk of the product, water, reaches the home via the tap.

The Signpost (SEE BOX 3)

So the decision maker now has a signpost, a name for what to look for: Symbiotic Technology. There are also good reasons for looking for it for, if products and processes that happen to have ecological superiority turn out to have the competitive edge, then it makes sense to consciously consider the environmental factor at the planning, research and development stages. And if a Symbiotic Technology does not have the edge under existing market conditions changes in legislation may present the opportunity. Indeed ecologically aware companies with a new Symbiotic Technology could actually consolidate their leading position

BOX 3

Symbiotic Technology

The key characteristics of the cleaner or "Symbiotic" technologies now appearing in many sectors, often for normal commercial reasons such as market appeal or greater cost effectiveness, are:

1. They are kinder to the environment,

2. They are developed and adopted primarily out of short term self interest, and

3. They act as a common denominator, simultaneously satisfying the differing objectives of commercial, environmental and government lobbies in the green debate.

by joining the lobby for stricter controls in a given area. Those involved with the older contentious conventional product or process could hardly argue when resisting the controls that there is not a valid alternative.

New opportunities through tighter legislation have appeared in the motor industry where catalytic converters and lean burn engines have become viable propositions in different regions in the face of stricter local lead emission controls. On the leisure front in the U.K. anglers' lead fishing weights have been blamed for lead poisoning in wildfowl. Lead-free weights were developed and presented with a market when it became evident that legislation could well be enacted to ban the lead weights because substitutes were now available.

The opportunities and strategies open to an ST innovator depend on the sector and existing market conditions. First, though, the Symbiotic Technology has to be found and the principle to defining one is identifying whether a product or process is kinder to the environment. To be thorough, this means looking beyond the boundaries of the organisation and its processes for any ecologically sensitive issues in the chains of supply or routes of sale or distribution. This "ST analysis" could have spinoff benefits in helping define alternative cost effective sources of supply or new markets for by-products. The technique itself is nothing new and it is possible to find where it has been applied (unnamed) because it made commercial sense: in one case a Scottish distillery reduced pollution problems and developed a profitable sideline through converting the spent wash from its stills to cattle cake.

The next five chapters are written by experts in the sectors concerned and they show where opportunities for environmentally kinder methods exist or have been seized. You can read them all or just those you think directly relevant to your particular interests.

The Industry chapter discusses the relevance of and some contemporary industrial views on the green factor and shows how Symbiotic Technologies are appearing in many, surprisingly diverse, sectors. "Waste" is then considered, being a consequence of many contemporary activities and, of course, cause of many well known problems. The chapter shows how waste issues can both adversely affect an organisation's interests as well as present new opportunities to those with sound policies and practices.

Energy conservation is discussed next in chapter 5 for, since its boost from the 70s oil crises, it has consistently displayed the main attribute of Symbiotic Technology, namely it is an ecologically sound industry that's grown primarily out of self interest (in cutting energy costs).

Agriculture and then finance in the developing situation are looked at as contributions by these sectors to environmental health are fundamental to our collective well-being. In chapter 7 the stark contrasts of the developing situation, where many individuals are allowed no margin for error, best illustrate how important it is for planners to consider the environmental factor. Also it shows vast sums of money affected, often adversely, by environmental factors.

All the reports show individuals and organisations benefiting or having the potential to benefit from what this chapter calls Symbiotic Technologies. And Symbiotic Technology is the decision maker's signpost to success in a world forced to be increasingly ecologically aware.

CHAPTER 3

INDUSTRY

JOHN ELKINGTON

WHATEVER THEY PRODUCE, whether it be cars, aerosols, tin cans, pesticides or power station equipment, business people now risk going out of business unless they make a serious attempt to understand the pressures which are beginning to 'green' their hard-won markets. At the same time, they also risk missing out on the many significant commercial opportunities which are now emerging for cleaner, quieter and more energy efficient technologies and products.

For the first time since the beginning of what Max Nicholson dubbed the 'environmental revolution', industry and commerce have the opportunity to present themselves as a credible part of the solution, rather than simply putting up with their image as the root cause of many of the world's most pressing environmental problems.

Some companies have already recognised this fact and are moving ahead rapidly to ensure that they are prepared for the impending changes in their business environment. Many more, of course, are doing no such thing. Playing an essentially defensive game in the face of constrained markets and intensifying international competition, they fail to recognise that many of their competitors are prepared to play a very different game.

Nowhere yet has this been clearer than at the World Industry Conference on Environmental Management (WICEM), which was organised by the United Nations Environment Programme (UNEP) and the International Chamber of Commerce (ICC).

Indeed, in retrospect, it was one of life's supreme ironies that the Bhopal disaster erupted into the world's headlines less than a month after WICEM drew to a close. The three day event, held in Versailles, had seen one industrialist after another standing up to explain what they were doing to meet the environmental challenge (1). And their audience, made up of over 500 senior people from industry, government and non-governmental organisations in 71 countries, were forcefully impressed by what they heard. In fact, and again in retrospect WICEM, hosted by the French Government, was an important symptom of a much wider transformation which is now taking hold of world industry.

Most of the industrialists present agreed with Mr. Robert Anderson, Chairman of the U.S. oil company Atlantic Richfield (ARCO), when he called WICEM "a landmark conference". But, while the fact that so many different corners of the environmental debate were represented was itself an achievement, their enthusiasm had had a great deal more to do with the underlying concept than with the event itself. There was, it emerged, overwhelmingly strong support for the idea that economic development and environmental protection should be, can be — and increasingly are — mutually supportive.

Much of this, of course, was old hat to environmental professionals. "Whether you talk of deforestation, or desertification, or soil erosion, or acid rain", said Baron de Rosen, former Director of UNEP's Industry and Environment Office, "there comes a moment when industry is called upon to provide, say, environmental monitoring equipment, earthmoving machinery, fertilisers, and other products or services. Since industrialists are going to be involved anyway, it makes sense to get them in at the beginning".

In short, industry must now be involved directly in the worldwide drive for 'sustainable development', in which economic and environmental objectives run in tandem. This, in fact, was a central message in the **World Conservation Strategy** (WCS) (2), launched in 1980, and it is interesting to note that the U.K. response to the WCS, entitled the **Conservation and Development Strategy for the U.K.** (3), recommended that industry and commerce should use the WCS itself as a market brief for the 1980s and 1990s. Many companies are beginning to do so (SEE BOX 1).

Environmentally-friendly technology, or 'Symbiotic Technology', will increasingly be what the market demands. This theme has also been developed by the new breed of bridging institutions, set up to establish links between business people and the sustainable development community. One of them, the World Resources Institute (WRI), based in Washington D.C., organised a panel of industrialists and

BOX 1

A RISING WIND FOR CLEAN SALES

"We cannot afford to be coy about selling our ideas on the world market", as CBI Director-General Sir Terence Beckett has put it. "The developed world is environmentally highly charged at the moment and if we don't take the opportunities which present themselves, our rivals most surely will". He might have added that, while Third World companies are usually unable to pay a massive premium for cleaner technologies and products, they certainly would buy them if they were available at a competitive price.

Britain, in fact, has been doing fairly well in the growing world environment business, exporting both products and services. In the water and effluent treatment sectors alone, the CBI has estimated that some 20,000 people are employed and British companies had about £250 million of orders in 1984, some 55-60% for export. Europe wide, it has been estimated that at least 1.25 million people are employed in the environmental industry.

One of the most important shop windows for such cleaner technologies and products has been the Pollution Abatement Technology Award scheme, which has highlighted a growing number of innovative approaches to cleaner,

quieter and more energy-efficient design. The award winners have ranged from major companies, such as BP and ICI, to very much smaller companies like British Earthworm Technology.

BP won its award for a new technique which uses safe chemical chemical reagents to solidify oil spills. The result: oilspills and slicks which once would have defied capture can now be peeled from the water like so many rubber mats. ICI, whose environmental policy is reproduced in Box 2, actually contrived to win two separate awards in a single year, one for its remarkable Electrodyne sprayer and one for a new enzyme technology which breaks down toxic cyanide.

The Electrodyne sprayer, which dramatically cuts the amount of pesticide needed to defend crops against pests, is a perfect illustration of how economic and ecological pressures can work in tandem. By electrically charging the droplets emerging from the unit's 'Bozzle', a combination bottle and nozzle, the Electrodyne sprayer enables a farmer to treat a hectare of crops with just one litre of pesticide, compared to the 200-400 litres normally used. Used with improved varieties of cowpea, for example, the Electrodyne can

BOX 1.

multiply food output ten-fold even in the semi-arid regions of Africa which have been so hard hit by drought and famine.

Other examples include money-making approaches to pollution control evolved by cider-makers H. P. Bulmer and the U.S. based company 3M — whose Pollution Prevention Pays (or 3P) programme has been an inspiration to all who believe that industry can simultaneously meet both environmental and economic objectives.

Bulmer, based in Hereford, developed a new process for treating hot, acidic still bottom effluents from a pectin extraction plant. This proved astonishingly efficient. It is based on the use of thermophilic, or heat-loving, bacteria grown in an anaerobic, or oxygen-free, digester. The capital cost of the plant was just £25,000. A conservative estimate of

the savings it generated in its first year: £30,000.

3M's 3P programme, meanwhile, had involved hundreds of separate projects. Between 1976 and 1982, for example, 3M mounted 832 projects to cut energy use and eliminated staggering quantities of pollution — in addition to saving the company £77 million. The initiative has continued as the next chapter (Waste) shows.

There have been a considerable number of other winners — and uncounted numbers of bright ideas have been submitted. But the scheme which perhaps best illustrated the way in which ecological technologies are beginning to worm their way into world markets was British Earthworm Technology's work on the use of earthworms to convert a wide range of waste materials into fertilisers and soil improvers. Nor does the story end there: the worms are suitable for feeding to animals and for use on fish farms.

H. P. BULMER'S AWARD WINNING AND VERY EFFICIENT PECTIN EFFLUENT
TREATMENT PLANT, ITS SMALL SIZE AN ADVANTAGE ON A SITE CROWDED BY
LARGE CIDER STORAGE TANKS (ABOVE).
(Photos: H. P. Bulmer Ltd.)

environmental specialists which later reported that "major market opportunities exist for pollution control equipment", while "new opportunities are emerging in renewable resource industries, including fuelwood plantation and other tree crops, brackish water aquaculture and unconventional energy projects. There may also be commercial opportunities in genetic engineering, remote sensing of natural resources, and data management in developing countries that are mutually beneficial". (4)

Japan's Success

Increasingly, environmental success will be a necessary — although clearly not yet sufficient — condition for economic success. Significantly some of the most striking success stories reported at WICEM came from Japan. Mr. Norishige Hasegawa, as Chairman of the giant Sumitomo Chemical Corporation and Vice-Chairman of Japan's Federation of economic organisations (KIEDANREN), described how most sectors of Japanese industry had undergone dramatic change because of environmental pressures. But, and there was hardly any need to labour the fact, he pointed out that Japanese industry had managed to remain highly competitive through this process of change.

In fact speaker after speaker noted that industries which had set out to cut down on pollution and waste, through recycling and the development of cleaner, low-waste technologies, had often been able to achieve greater profitability than competitors that had stuck with older, more polluting technologies.

"The best solution", said Dr. Otto Koch, a Director of the West German chemical company Bayer AG, "clearly lies in new, environmentally-safe technologies with which products can be manufactured without any significant waste generation, or such that it is easily manageable. This solution of the future will nevertheless require one or two decades for the research, development and industrial start-up. Environmentalists, journalists and politicians without any scientific or technical back-up do not appreciate this fact". In some senses though he did his company an unintentional disservice — in that it was already installing such technologies to protect the Rhine and North Sea environments (5).

As far as the press were concerned, however, the initial reaction of the press corps was one of wry disbelief. "What our readers will ask themselves", insisted the man from the Associated Press, "is what does it all mean? Will WICEM really change industrial priorities? Do all industrialists, or even many of them, operate — or even think — like those who have spoken here?"

There is no simple answer to these questions, except to say that there have been tremendous changes in the professionalism with which many companies address the environmental agenda. But there remain undoubted problems. Even the developed countries, as Continental Group Chairman Mr. Bruce Smart argued, are often still "operating from a comprehensive background of ignorance".

However, the most forceful pleas for better information transfers inevitably came from the The Third World. As Mr. Anil Agarwal, Director of the Centre for Science and the Environment, based in New Delhi, India, put it, "if you want sustainable development, and if you want to develop your natural resources in an environmentally sound manner, you are going to need extraordinary information resources". Again, the call is starting to go out to industry.

Industry: An Untapped Reservoir

The key point highlighted by WICEM was that industry itself is now an increasingly important source of the information, technology and other resources needed for sustainable development. Perhaps the most succinct summary of the way industry is now increasingly seen from the environmental side of the fence came from Mr. William Ruckelshaus, then still Administrator at the U.S. Environmental Protection Agency. A widely respected industrialist, recruited originally from the timber products company Weyerhaeser, Mr. Ruckelshaus caught the mood of the moment when he described the private sector as "a vast reservoir of untapped creative talent". Despite tight budgetary constraints, he said, "this is where many solutions will be generated".

And then came Bhopal. Inevitably the series of accidents and mishaps which proceeded to dog Union Carbide, both in India and in the United States, led some people to query whether WICEM's conclusions were worth the paper they were printed on? But as further details emerged about why the accident had happened, it became clear that if Union Carbide had adopted the sort of approach proposed by WICEM, the chances are that over 2,000 people would have been spared their grim fate.

Union Carbide, meanwhile, was struggling to improve its handling of the health, safety and environmental aspects of its business. It appointed a new Vice-President for health, safety and environmental affairs, and Chairman Mr. Warren Anderson said the company's goal would be to "achieve and maintain a level of health, safety and environmental protection in all our operations that is second to none". But if the industrial presentations made at WICEM were anything to go by, that could prove to be a very tall order.

BOX 2

Doing More With Less

Industrialists may hope that the environmental pressure will recede, says ICI Chairman Sir John Harvey-Jones, but they will almost certainly be disappointed.

"I think it's a continuing situation", he stresses. "The rate of climb may vary, but I think it is an inevitable trend. First of all, our understanding of the environment, of the trigger effects in the environment, is growing the whole time. And as you find new cause and effect links it is right and proper that you should deal with the resulting problems. Secondly we are moving further and further into a situation where people have more and more leisure. People appreciate more and more the opportunity to enjoy the environment as part of their quality of life, so the pressures are not going to get any less".

Many of today's environmental problems, however, are even more complex than those which yesterday's industrialists had to face. "Certainly our biggest problem is in establishing the links between cause and effect", Sir John notes. "The outstanding example of this, of course, is acid rain. Although quite plainly some linkages have been established, the process is still not fully understood. And, understandably, we are fairly windy of over-reacting until we have reasonably clear evidence that what we are doing is causing problems —

because nearly everything you do environmentally costs money".

But that is not the end of the story, he stresses. "Even if the evidence is contradictory", he suggests, "if there are alternative technologies which are economically viable they should be used. The only case where we should be careful is if no viable alternative exists. Take aerosols. The difficulty with aerosols, of course, is that when you mention the word most people think of air-fresheners or hair-sprays, yet there are a hell of a lot of applications where aerosols do things you cannot get done in any other way".

So should industry be doing more to present its side of the argument? "Yes", agrees Sir John, "but you can't advertise your way out of environmental issues. If you spent a lot on advertising, people will say you must be rolling in money — and imagine you must have something to hide. We have got to use a less dramatic, more persistent approach".

And what message should industry be trying to communicate? "Our most important task", says Sir John, "is to get more and more out of less. That is the industrialist's mission. And actually we are getting pretty good at it. Incidentally, too, that's not because we are boy scouts. It's for bloody good business reasons".

ICI's environmental policy runs as follows:

All industrial activity has an impact on the environment. It is the policy of ICI to manage its activities so as to ensure that they are acceptable to the community and to reduce adverse effects to a practicable minimum. This policy recognises that the environment is able to absorb certain man-made effects, and is thus a resource to be used as well as one to be conserved.

In order to implement this policy, ICI will:

FOR ALL ITS ACTIVITIES

— Co-operate fully with the relevant authorities in meeting its legal obligations.

— Participate expertly in the discussion of relevant environmental issues, with a view to ensuring that an appropriate balance is maintained between care for the environment and the benefit arising from the Company's activities in each of the communities in which it operates.

FOR NEW ACTIVITIES

— Assess in advance, as far as possible, the environmental effects of any new developments.

— Take steps to minimise any adverse effects on man or the environment.

— Have particular regard for the preservation of important habitats, avoiding adverse effects on rare or endangered species of flora or fauna.

FOR ITS PRODUCTS

— Provide the information necessary to enable the Company's products to be properly used, stored and disposed of, so as to avoid unacceptable effects on man or the environment.

FOR ITS PROCESSES

— Provide the necessary information to enable the Company's processes, when under licence, to be operated without unacceptable effects to man or the environment.

Searchlight of Public Scrutiny

The Bhopal disaster, coupled with such other pressing environmental issues such as acid rain, has ensured that the environmental pressure on industry will, if anything, increase. Leading industrialists, like ICI's Sir John Harvey-Jones (SEE BOX 2), recognise this fact — and are increasingly acting upon it.

"Most political commentators seem to agree that concern for the environment is one of the growth issues of the future", as BP (British Petroleum) Managing Director Mr. Peter Cazelet put it during a conference held in Cambridge by the U.K. Centre for Economic and Environmental Development (CEED) (6). As CEED Chairman Sir Arthur Norman, also Chairman of De La Rue, summed up the prospect, even the most environmentally sensitive industries must accept that in many areas "the searchlight of public scrutiny burns more intensely than ever".

The real need now, as Sir Peter Parker put it (SEE BOX 3), is to bring the environmental debate to the "flashpoint of managerial action". In fact some innovative ventures have already produced real results. There are a growing number of fora in which people in industry can work with those who are concerned to ensure that economic growth is not achieved at the expense of environmental quality. A number of industrialists also helped prepare the industrial component of the **Conservation and Development Programme for the U.K.** And, under the auspices of CEED, environmentalists, conservationists and representatives of the relevant Government departments met industrial biotechnologists to discuss the environmental implications and applications of biotechnology (7). Such bridge-building must increase.

Ultimately, however, technologies — indeed whole industries are subject to the laws of natural selection in much the same way as are animal or plant species. If their business environment changes, they must evolve or risk going under. Thinking about the environmental prospect is often a useful way of catalysing thinking about impending challenges in other fields. Like the design process, it can provoke productive lateral thinking.

On the public relations level, there is every reason to believe that the public is more receptive to the message that industry — and technology — can help solve the world's environmental problems. If industry is seen to be tackling such problems, it may help much more broadly, in marketing, for example, and staff recruitment.

It is vital that industry recognises this fact, not just for the sake of the economic viability of industrial companies but for the sake of all our futures. For one thing is certain: as we begin to exhaust the wealth of North Sea oil and gas, so we must urgently look for new ways of harnessing the country's renewable resources — and most particularly its human skills and ingenuity. We may not be a model of sustainable development, but the building blocks are unquestionably there.

BOX 3

Flashpoints of Managerial Action

"The business response to the environmental challenge is still in practice, and I fear in general, uneven, uncoordinated and unconvincing", as Sir Peter Parker recently put it. As chairman of the Rockware Group and of the British Institute of Management (BIM), he was concerned that the environmental debate should be brought down to "the flashpoint of managerial action". But he was in "no doubt that the environment is now at last a sticking point on the agenda for management in the eighties".

Speaking at a conference on sustainable developments organised by the Centre for Economic and Environmental Development (CEED), Sir Peter was not entirely convinced by the definitions he had been offered of 'sustainable development'. "There is an evident lack of clarity", was the way he put it. "The debate is blurred. The definition of sustainable economic development is still likely to prove elusive for a harassed management dealing with problems of profit, jobs and shareholders. Frankly management is learning by doing".

Noting that the winners of awards under the Business & Industry Panel for the Environment and the Pollution Abatement Technology Award schemes "have turned out to be pace-makers in profitability as well", he proposed ten environmental commandments for management. While apologising for having "fallen into that most fashionable of all managerial traps, dressing up ideas in a check-list", he stressed that "there is urgent need to simplify management ideas on this 360 degree challenge of the environment".

Briefly stated, his ten commandments were these:

1. **Define your Policy:** It is vital to get the commitment of a company's Board if environmental programmes are to succeed (see ICI's policy in Box 2).

2. **Draw Up An Action Programme:** This must stem from Board policy and be part of the continuing corporate planning process. Companies like BP state quite categorically that all new products, projects, activities and acquisitions should be assessed against environmental criteria.

3. **Structure Your Organisation:** There must be a carefully thought through organisational structure, establishing exactly who is accountable for what. "There is always the danger, I recognize", said Sir Peter, "that a Director of Environment over-specializes the responsibility. However, I have found that there is always a need for a champion of any product, especially at the innovation stage. The risks of some specialization have to be measured — and, usually, taken to get things moving".

4. Review Your Financial Systems: Budgetary and financial control systems are as essential as in any other areas of business. The returns on projects should be exposed. Annual accounts provide an opportunity to report to all shareholders — although not all environmental benefits can be demonstrated in such accounting processes. "Some will emerge in industrial and public relations", Sir Peter stressed: "less quantifiable, but no less important".

5. Allocate Technological Resources: Quoting the 3M Pollution Prevention Pays programme (see Box 1) as a prime example, Sir Peter underscored the fact that the technology must be made available to match the company's policy. The 3P programme, he said, "shows what can be achieved by product reformulation, process modification, equipment redesign and the recovery of waste materials for re-use". In the car industry, to take another example, environmental considerations must be a central component in the drive for product quality. Tomorrow's car will need to be cleaner, more fuel-efficient and longer lasting.

6. Spell Out Your Policy:
Everyone in the company must be made aware of its environmental policies and programmes. "I take the line that people in our companies are not just employees, not just trade unionists: they are citizens at work", said Sir Peter, "and as such are interested in facts which may have life or death importance to the company". These now include questions relating to environmental quality.

7. Educate and Train: Education and training programmes must alert people to society's evolving environmental priorities. Because business schools and other training insitutions have failed to develop environmental case study approaches for their students, "a generation of trained managers have 'got away'. More must be done to gather case-histories and effectively disseminate best practice. A modern manager must not think of sustainable development as an optional extra: 'You mean I have to think about this and my job too?'" Environment is now an inescapable part of industry's mission.

8 Connect: "Management is not an island". It must be in close touch with opinion leaders and those who shape policy and legislation. The environment, said Sir Peter, is "too important to be left to politicians".

9. Monitor the International Scene: "Standards are being set, quite properly in my view, not only regionally but globally. The environmental priority will turn out to be indivisible". Industry, in consequence, must keep in touch with what is happening around the world which might shape industry's environmental agenda.

10. Get Management's Message Across: "In the evolution of the environmental priority, management did not lead: it was pulled, it was reacting. The environmental debate has begun and industry must have a voice in it. Management, not slow to see the way the cookie — and the world — crumbles, can see that ultimately it, too, could be an endangered species".

CHAPTER 4

WASTE

MAREK MAYER

THE WORLD'S PLASTICS INDUSTRY will have to introduce a new dimension to its product development stategy if its hope of making major inroads into the vehicle manufacturing market is not to be strangled at birth, senior chemical industry executives were told at a conference in London in October 1985. "We must assume that in 10 to 15 years from now," they were warned, "it will no longer be possible to dump the plastic componets being installed in cars today as they come out of industrial shredders." Until the plastics industry places environmental considerations at the forefront of its thinking and devises practical methods to recycle plastic vehicle conponents, no car manufacturer will be prepared to take the risk of investing in new production plant geared to maximising plastics usage.

The impress of the Green Party of West Germany, from where the speaker hailed, was clearly evident. But he was not, as might be supposed, a member of the Greens, but Dr Wolfgang Habbel, the Chairman of Audi AG. Yet anyone in his audience who harboured hopes of an easier ride outside the German market would have done well to listen to a speech that same month by Britain's Minister of State for the Environment, William Waldegrave.

"Complacency about environmental protection in British industry", the Minister said, "will cost it dear in terms of lost business. Both at home and in the markets of our environmentally conscious European neighbours and those of North America, the successful companies will be those which have developed low-waste, low-pollution technologies". Equally, Mr Waldegrave warned, "we can increasingly expect the developing world, quite rightly, to insist on evironmentally sound products and environmentally friendly technology."

The message to industry is clear. The first phase of the environmental movement which began in the late 1960s, and generally involved costly and often unproductive investments in end-of-pipe pollution abatement technologies, is now tapering off. The emphasis of the second wave, which became visible among the more farsighted companies in the mid-1970s but which has still to take root across industry, will be on designing out waste disposal and pollution problems at source from both new processes and products. Happily, experience to date suggests that companies which swim with the tide will often benefit with improved sales prospects, better productivity, and new employment — and avoid the unwanted publicity which can come of confrontations with the environmental lobby.

Banking on Bottle Recycling

The development of glass recycling in Britain is a telling case study in how an industry which initially met the environmental movement head-on has slowly been converted to its case. In the early 1970s, the campaign launched by Friends of the Earth against the one-trip glass container as an outstanding example of profligacy with natural resources was greeted by the container manufacturers with a vigorous PR campaign and then, as the prospect of EEC recycling legislation came into sight, with the launch of the "Bottle Bank" scheme in 1977.

Lack of pressure from central government, inadequate interest among many local authorities, and the downturn in the glass container industry itself were among the reasons why the Bottle Bank scheme remained largely a cosmetic exercise well into the 1980s. In 1984, Britain — recycling just 9% of its discarded bottles — was still at the very bottom of western Europe's glass recycling league, while several countries were achieving a recycling rate of 30% or more.

That same year, however, one of Britian's top glass container manufacturers, Rockware, hived off its existing recycling activities to an autonomous company, Rockware Reclamation. The subsidiary's objective is to turn recycling of all kinds of packaging materials into profit-making ventures in their own right. As George Maund, the new company's Managing Director, explained in 1985, "Rockware's involvement with Bottle Banks began largely as an attempt to overcome public objections to the non-returnable bottle. Not everybody felt at the time that glass recovery would become so important to the industry. But with the continuing rise in energy and raw material prices, we now see cullet as a very valuable raw material — and want as much of it as we can lay our hands on."

By investing in additional Bottle Banks and extra publicity for the scheme, Rockware Reclamation increased the amount of glass passing through their cullet processing plant in Knottingley, West Yorkshire, from 38,500 tonnes in 1984 to some 50,000 tonnes in 1985. The result was a net saving of at least £200,000 per year in the form of reduced energy bills for Rockware's glass-melting furnaces — a vital contribution to higher productivity at a time when the glass industry is under unprecedented pressure from metal and plastic container manufacturers. The aim by the end of 1986 is to increase the recycling rate to 70,000 tonnes, the limit of the Knottingley plant's capacity.

Other packaging wastes will form the building blocks for further expansion of Rockware Reclamation's recycling business. In mid-1985, it launched the first commercial trial of a reverse vending machine which gives consumers $\frac{1}{2}$p for every spent aluminium can they deposit. Further machines will follow at the company's Bottle Bank sites, helping to keep down collection overheads. But George Maund expects that recycling of plastics packaging will become the largest element in the company's activities within the next few years.

Linking Growth with Conservation

Recent developments in the U.S.A. suggest, indeed, that there is substantial scope for creating profitable businesses and employment from recycling at least some forms of plastic packaging. There, market penetration of the new polyethylene terephthalate (PET) soft drinks bottle began earliest, rising from a zero base in 1975 to reach almost 200,000 tonnes in 1981. By 1984, when PET sales had risen to 300,000 tonnes, some 45,000 tonnes were being reclaimed and processed for re-use.

Worldwide, PET is fast becoming one of the biggest success stories in the history of the plastics industry. Although PET only began to displace glass and metal containers outside the U.S.A. in 1979, global sales had risen to 465,000 tonnes in 1984, and are expected virtually to double again to 880,000 tonnes by 1990. But a goodly quantity may have to be shaved off those projections unless PET manufacturers heed the warnings they have already received from several European governments: "develop practicable methods of recycling PET or face the prospect of being excluded from our markets".

Unlike glass bottles — which can be cleaned-up and colour-separated relatively easily, and made into new bottles in a conventional glass-making furnace — PET is not a recycling "natural". Consumers can easily confuse it with the many other forms of plastics packaging now on the market. The product itself may be coated with materials which interfere with the recycling process. And, since the PET and drinks industries are unwilling to accept recycled PET for re-use in bottles or other forms of packaging, different — preferably high-value — outlets have to be found for the recycled product.

Europe's largest PET manufacturer, ICI Fibres, sensed early on that PET's full market potential would not be realised unless these constraints were overcome. Although ICI do not themselves intend to move into recycling, they have made their considerable technical resources available to firms thinking of doing so — and have offered to pull their own in-house waste PET off the market to make room for the recycled variety.

What appears to be an important breakthrough in PET recycling technology was unveiled in September 1985 by a small Midlands firm, PlasTech. In a joint venture with a West German company, Amberger Kaolinwerke, PlasTech have advanced PET recycling techniques to the point where the end-product has a purity of up to 99.98% — adequate to open up a range of new high-value end-uses in injection and blow-moulding, reinforced engineering plastics, and many others. Late in 1985, PlasTech were also expecting to announce that they had devised a way of removing polyvinyl dichloride coatings from PET bottles — thereby eliminating another barrier to recovery of pure PET.

It is on developments such as these that new recycling ventures, and export opportunities for innovative companies such as PlasTech, could be built. The question which ICI, PlasTech, Rockware Reclamation and several other firms with an interest in seeing PET recycling take off were asking in 1985 was whether drinks manufacturers and retailers who are benefiting from the lower weight and unbreakability of PET bottles will play their part in ensuring that it does. In Britain, the issue is unlikely to be settled unless the Government firmly signals that it expects all the parties involved to contribute to the development of a new recycling industry. It could do worse than study the examples set in the U.S.A., where PET recycling rates are approaching 80% in the nine states which impose mandatory deposits on beverage containers, and in West Germany, where Coca-Cola has introduced its own deposit system after being told by the federal government that the introduction of PET bottles was not acceptable in the absence of a recycling scheme.

Waste – The Untapped Resource

Recycling of materials as different as oils, solvents, metals, textiles, plastics and paper is, of course, already an established industry in its own right. Materials worth £1,800 million are reclaimed in Britain every year, keeping some 20,000 people in employment in the process. But the total, according to the House of Commons Trade and Industry Committee's 1984 report "The Wealth of Waste", could be increased by at least a further £750 million per year, given the right degree of co-operation from central government, local authorities and industry.

The message is taking a long time to get through. In the meantime, as the U.S. Institute of Scrap Iron and Steel (ISIS) pointed out in 1985, innovations which promise to bring a whole host of new plastic and metal composite materials onto the market could well impede part of the existing recycling effort. Metal parts plated with cadmium which can be emitted from metal recovery furnaces as fume and contribute to the build-up in the environment of this toxic, persistent and bioaccumulative metal; new high-strength steels containing rare metals which, once they enter the scrap chain, are no longer assets but contaminants which restrict steel recycling except to low value outlets; containers of sodium azide to inflate the air bags which are to be fitted to some new U.S. vehicles from 1986 to protect their occupants in road accidents, but which could cause explosions in scrap processing plants — these are just three of the examples cited by ISIS of the unthinking introduction of impediments to material recycling at the product design stage. Instead, ISIS argues, design engineers and manufacturing executives should begin treating recyclability on a par with the appearance and durability of their products. Even relatively simple changes in design or material specifications can often make the difference between efficient recycling and the creation of unrecoverable — sometimes hazardous — wastes for which dumping is the only management option.

Profiting from Pollution Prevention

Designers and decision-makers in industry may, until now, have been able to shrug off responsibility for the ultimate fate of their products simply because the cost of disposing of them does not feature in corporate balance sheets. The same, however, cannot be said of material wastage at the production stage, where the cost of treating or disposing of gaseous, liquid or solid residues from the manufacturing process can be substantial.

Environmental legislation introduced in the industrialised countries since the early 1970s has undoubtedly prompted companies to take a harder look during the process design stage at the scope for eliminating or reducing these overheads. Yet there are still few firms who are doing so quite as systematically and successfully as the multinational 3M Company of Minnesota.

In 1975, 3M introduced a "Pollution Prevention Pays" — or 3P — Programme across all their operating companies. Its goal was nothing less than a radical overhaul of the existing approach to eliminating pollution, which at the time was based largely on removal and treatment of wastes after they had been created by a manufacturing process. This end-of-pipe approach, 3M concluded, took scarce capital away from productive investments; sometimes failed to eliminate the emission completely; often generated large quantities of secondary wastes which had to be disposed of at a cost; and generally required energy inputs which, again, channelled funds away from the company's mainstream activities.

As of 1975, the emphasis shifted to the prevention of pollution at source. Under the 3P Programme, all 3M employees are encouraged by means of awards and other incentives to examine operations for which they are responsible for their polluting potential, and to contribute new methods of preventing or reducing it — whether by product reformulation, process modifications, the re-design of equipment, or the recovery of waste materials for re-use. The same philosophy is applied during the development of new products, processes or equipment. "Early awareness of possible pollution problems", as 3M explain, "can eliminate the considerable effort and investment which may be required for later redesign or retrofitting of pollution control equipment." (SEE BOX).

3M's achievements since 1975 have been nothing if not impressive. With 1,528 projects implemented under the 3P Programme by the end of 1984, the company calculates that it has saved itself $235 million by delaying or eliminating the need for add-on pollution control equipment, by saving on raw material, energy and operating costs, and by retaining sales of products which might otherwise have had to be taken off the market as environmentally unacceptable. Equally important, the cumulative impact of 3M's manufacturing activities on the environment between 1975 and 1984 was reduced by the elimination of 98,000 tonnes of air pollutants, 10,500 tonnes of water pollutants, 1,440 million gallons of waste water, and just over 150,000 tonnes of sludges and solid wastes.

The 3P Programme is undoubtedly exceptional, and probably for that reason is commonly greeted with a number of sceptical stock responses by industry. Pollution prevention is by no means always profitable, and dispensing with end-of-pipe treatment is an environmentalists'

BOX

Little and Large in the Pollution Prevention Pays (3P) Programme

One advantage of having systematic procedures and a formal employee education and incentive scheme to identify waste-saving opportunities, 3M's experience suggests, is that small, technically unsophisticated projects which might otherwise be overlooked are constantly being implemented. Employees at the company's Gorseinon plant in Wales, for example, suggested that carbon black should be supplied in polythene bags rather than paper sacks. The new sacks could be fed directly into a raw material mix, improving the working environment as well as saving the company an annual £5,000 in sack disposal costs.

But many other pollution prevention projects demand a considerable input of technical and marketing resources. A 3M factory in Minnesota which manufactures magnetic oxides for recording products eliminated the need to invest $1 million in pollution control equipment by separating an ammonia-rich waste stream from millions of gallons of other effluent and passing it through a new vapour compression evaporator to produce fertilser-grade ammonium sulphate. The evaporator cost $1.5 million — but the extra cost was offset in just over three years by fertiliser sales worth $150,000 per annum.

pipedream — both points being readily conceded by 3M. Industry, the argument continues, is constantly looking for all possible means to improve productivity, and the reduction of pollution and raw material wastage is no exception; 3M are just more publicity-conscious about this than other companies. Then again, less wasteful processes may be available but will not be introduced until the economic incentive — be it higher raw material or energy prices, or stricter anti-pollution or waste disposal regulations — becomes strong enough.

Missed Opportunities

All these arguments have more than a grain of truth in them. There is, however, a considerable body of evidence now available which shows that industry is by no means as effective at identifying and capitalising on financially attractive opportunities for reducing wastage as it might sometimes believe.

ICI's Mond Division, for example, has spent more than £20 million since 1975 on reducing mercury discharges from its chlor-alkali production facilities at Runcorn, Cheshire. The reduction means that mercury concentrations in the local environment are now a very long way below those likely to pose a hazard to human health — but, as ICI point out, the value of the recovered mercury covers only a small fraction of the £2 million spent annually on improved effluent treatment.

Yet, in the same manufacturing complex, it required prodding from the water authority for a reduction in ammonia discharges to a nearby canal from a chlorinated solvents plant for ICI to identify a profitable waste reduction opportunity. A process change implemented at "trivial" expense, according to ICI, brought annual savings of £45,000 in ammonia costs, £35,000 in other reagent purchases, and £200,000 in effluent treatment expenditures. Without the process modification, the company would have needed a new effluent treatment plant costing £600,000.

Then there was the local resident with an exceptional sense of smell whose complaints about low-level odour emissions from a polyester resin plant in Northamptonshire brought financial benefits to the operator, Scott Bader. Odourous emissions from various sources were fed, together with distillation residues from resin production which had previously been landfilled, to a new incinerator equipped with a heat recovery unit. The results? Savings of £200 per day in waste transport and landfill costs, process steam for the factory, a pollution problem solved, and the opportunity to use materials which would otherwise have been environmentally unacceptable.

Tighter regulations and public complaints, in other words, can prove to be less an unwanted economic burden than a positive external stimulus towards the achievement of improved industrial efficiency. In the same way, the history of the U.K. Waste Materials Exchange suggests that intervention by an outside agency can benefit companies by revealing cost-saving outlets for unwanted process residues.

Exchanging Wastes

Established with Government assistance at Warren Spring Laboratory in 1974, the Exchange brought together companies looking for outlets for their wastes with firms able to re-use secondary materials. By 1979, it had facilitated the reclamation of wastes worth at least £8.5 million, with particularly high exchange rates being achieved for acids, alkalis, solvents, polymers, and paper, leather and textile wastes. These transactions also saved industry an aggregate £1–1.5 million in waste disposal costs — all for operating expenditures which totalled £187,000. Yet despite its undoubted national benefits, the Exchange was wound up in 1979 because, predictably, insufficient numbers of industrial sponsors were prepared to pay the subscriptions needed to put it on a self-funding footing.

In much the same way, West Midlands County Council has been proving that information can be an invaluable asset in the pursuit of improved efficiency in industrial waste management. The Council's own waste exchange, set up early in 1983 and managed by staff in its Pollution Control Division, helped local industry to savings of £25,000 in its first year of operation. Typical examples of successful transactions included a printing company which was able to have 1,800 gallons of waste methylated spirits removed free of charge for incineration at an agricultural establishment, saving it £320 per year in disposal charges; and the re-use of paint thinners from an equipment cleaning operation in two outlets which brought a vehicle manufacturer a £1,500 reduction in his annual waste disposal bill.

Information of another sort is essential if industry is to take full advantage of available, cost-effective waste reduction opportunities, according to several studies of the diffusion of "clean" technologies by the Birmingham environmental consultancy, ECOTEC. Small and medium sized companies, ECOTEC has found, are often reluctant to introduce even low-cost, rapid pay-back measures to reduce material wastage and avert pollution because they lack the technical expertise needed to assess their equipment suppliers' claims.

Industry, ECOTEC's studies have suggested, can only do so much on its own to reduce the environmental impact of its processes. A positive corporate commitment to environmental protection, backed by systematic procedures and employee incentives for identifying profitable waste reduction opportunities, are two essential ingredients. But so, too, are pressure from regulatory authorities for a gradual improvement in environmental standards, and officially-sponsored research, information and training programmes directed at those sectors which currently lack the resources needed to implement waste reduction programmes on their own.

Notwithstanding the introduction of all possible waste reduction measures, wastes will inevitably continue to arise for disposal. For some industries, the achievement of acceptable standards of disposal is now a priority in their efforts to convince the public that they care for the environment — and none more so than the chemical industry, which in 1985 issued the most detailed industrial waste management guidelines hitherto published by any sector through its European Council of Chemical Manufacturers' Federations (CEFIC).

Management Systems for Hazardous Wastes

Equally applicable outside the chemical industry, the guidelines emphasise that minimising waste generation should be a priority consideration at all stages of process development and plant design, and that senior management should take responsibility for ensuring that this is done. Company management should also ensure that all economically feasible steps are taken to recover materials from the waste stream, with responsibility for reviewing recycling opportunities being assigned to a technically competent person. Similarly, a nominated manager, with access to sound technical knowledge and full awareness of legislative requirements, should be made responsible for safe and effective disposal of all waste generated. He or she, CEFIC recommend, should take steps — including periodic visits to disposal sites — to ensure that the company's waste disposal contractors are adopting technically and environmental sound disposal practices.

Whatever the performance of the chemical industry may be, there is ample evidence in Britain that industrial waste management practices in general, and hazardous waste disposal practices in particular, are currently falling well short of these guidelines. In 1982, for example a study of day-to-day hazardous waste management practices among almost 300 companies in Scotland revealed that just 9% assign this function to specialists in health, safety, waste management or environmental protection with another 42% devolving responsibility in this area onto production, technical or engineering staff. In the remaining 49%, staff in the general administrative or sales, stores and purchasing sections handled this function — a practice, the study concluded, which "could be positively inconsistent with informed and responsible decision making and an acceptable sense of priorities."

Then there was the disturbing first report of the Hazardous Waste Inspectorate. Published in June 1985, it recorded that a combination of poor enforcement of existing legislation, widespread non-observance of official waste management guidelines, and the existence of waste disposal operators who were prepared to drive down prices and substantial numbers of waste generators who were prepared to accept them, had resulted in a downward spiral in disposal standards. "All too many major hazardous waste disposal sites have been seen", the report said, "which exude an atmosphere of total dereliction and decay, are under-equipped, under-manned, and are operated with a notable lack of professionalism."

And what of it? One consequence was spelled out in the Inspectorate's report: that Britain is perilously close to finding itself without adequate specialist disposal facilities — and particularly incinerators — which had lost business as a result of the misrouting of hazardous wastes to landfills. That may not be a problem for industry as a whole, but the experience of 1972 — when the Deposit of Poisonous Waste Act was rushed through Parliament in a few days following the illegal dumping of cyanide wastes — suggests that it would not take many incidents involving hazardous waste to bring massive public pressure for stricter legislation and tighter operational standards. Too much short-term accounting, in other words, and British industry as a whole could find itself gradually losing the cheap landfill disposal option which it has enjoyed for many decades.

Picking Winners

The financial problems with which most of Britain's specialist hazardous waste disposal facilities are currently wrestling are a case study in — depending on one's viewpoint — the penalties of basing investments on over-optimistic market projections, or alternatively the commercial consequences of a failure by the regulatory authorities to force a gradual improvement in industrial waste management standards. Picking winners in the waste management business may be an occupation more than usually dependent on other people's decisions — but there are, on the other hand, companies which have displayed exceptional acumen in sensing the market opportunities which will come of public demands for higher environmental standards.

Engineering consultants V Lawson Associates were shrewd enough to begin looking for diversification of their existing business at the height of the 1972 economic boom. Despite the fact that the company's review of potential future growth areas spanned the oil shock of 1973, energy-related projects were not, in the event, selected for detailed investigation. "While there were fears that energy prices would continue to escalate, we concluded", recalls its Chairman Victor Lawson, "that material recycling and recovery would show the highest profits in the years to come."

The reasoning was straightforward. In most of the developed world, between a quarter and half a tonne of solid waste is discarded per head of population; a similar and — as more sewage treatment plants are built — growing quantity of sewage sludge is generated for disposal. Yet disposal of these wastes, the company foresaw, was likely to become more costly as landfill capacity for refuse near the main population centres became exhausted, and as sewage sludge had to be carried longer distances to outlets on land or at sea. Both wastes, at the same time, were a largely untapped reservoir of valuable secondary resources.

A decade's development work — now taken over by WMC Resource Recovery — has resulted in a process in which the two wastes are brought together for treatment to yield a variety of saleable products. Materials such as plastics, glass and metals are separated from the refuse stream for further processing before its organic constituents are mixed with sewage sludge and passed into a novel design of anaerobic digester. Output from the digester is a conditioned sludge which can be further processed into three different materials, dependent on local market demand: a horticultural peat-like product, a fibrous residue which can be used in board manufacture, or a fuel suitable for use in its own right or after blending with coal. In addition, enough gas is generated during the digestion process to power the entire operation. The process has been designed to accommodate the wide variations in refuse composition encountered across Europe, increasing its appeal in Mediterranean countries which are in the midst of massive sewage infrastructure investments.

Legislative Pressures

Interest in WMC's process is high among Britain's water authorities, one of which, Thames Water, has provided room at a sewage works for construction of a series of full-scale modules which will treat 360 tonnes of refuse and 780 cubic metres of sewage sludge per day. The explanation is not hard to find: the water authorities, producing between them some 35 million tonnes of sludge every year, are finding that their main disposal outlets are under increasing pressure from EEC environmental legislation.

Sewage sludge disposal practices in Britain rely uncomfortably on just three principal disposal routes. Dumping at sea takes about 30% of the total. With the exception of a small operation by Eire, no other EEC country now dumps sludge at sea, leaving Britain open to accusations that it is abusing a common international resource. Sludge spreading on agricultural land takes approximately 45% of the total, but this disposal route, too, may be limited by EEC legislation seeking to restrict the land disposal of metal-contaminated sludge and to reduce the risk of bacterial contamination of livestock. Another 22% is dumped on sacrificial sites on land, with the residue being incinerated or used in land reclamation projects.

Warnings that these practices could not continue indefinitely began to be sounded in 1981, when a senior Ministry of Agriculture official and the then Chairman of the Oslo Commission — the international pollution regulatory body for the North Sea — advised that "there should be a revolution in our attitudes so that, through technical advances, sewage sludge comes to be recognised as a valuable by-product for recycling instead of as a waste product for which disposal routes have to be found." But, even with the possibility that a ban on sea dumping alone might cost it £30 million per year in extra disposal costs, the water industry has been slow to respond to these international pressures. In 1981, 95% of Britain's £1 million R & D expenditure on sewage sludge was dedicated to defending the two main disposal outlets or improving the efficiency of sludge treatment.

The balance has begun to shift, albeit slowly. Studies now under way at the Water Research Centre (WRC) are aimed at creating new outlets for sewage sludge in derelict and mineral land reclamation, in composting with straw to form a soil additive, and as a means of boosting yields of energy-rich gas when sludge is disposed of with refuse in landfills. Beyond that, as a WRC study has suggested, sewage sludge contains an annual £200 million worth of materials such as fats and proteins, together with components which could form the basis of fuel or horticultural peat production on a large scale.

The evolution of Britain's sewage sludge disposal strategy could take one of two directions. Britain could either maintain its insistence that, on scientific grounds, there is nothing environmentally harmful about its sea and land disposal practices — but the penalty would be another blot on its already tarnished environmental reputation. Alternatively, Britain could invest in the long term R & D needed to open up one or more of the potential avenues for sewage sludge utilisation. The lures would be revenue from sales of sludge-based products, a reduction in the environmental damage caused by the extraction of minerals which they could displace from the market, and new export opportunities which, for the time being, only the foresight of firms like WMC Resource Recovery are creating.

Spoiling an Industry's Future

Sewage sludge, straw, and domestic and industrial wastes — for all these there is at least the prospect that, properly managed, they will not pose insuperable hazards to the environment. More than that, considerable businesses are likely to be built around new ideas for cashing in on their resource value. Yet there is one industry — coal mining and utilisation — whose waste disposal problems are likely to become so intractable in the not too distant future as to pose a distinct threat to its continued existence.

Consider the following statistics. In 1982, when the last official mineral working and derelict land surveys were carried out, colliery spoil heaps had rendered derelict more than 12,500 acres of land. On almost another 20,000 acres, dumping of colliery spoil had recently ceased but the land had not yet been reclaimed. Add to that some 500 acres every year for spoil tips at present rates of deep mine output, and a further 5,000 acres of land — not all of it by any means later reclaimed to its original productive capacity — taken each year by Britain's expanding opencast coal industry, and the environmental impact of coal mining begins to look fairly substantial. To that, moreover, should be added the land taken by the Central Electricity Generating Board (CEGB) to dump around 9 million tonnes of fuel ash from its coal-fired power stations every year.

Then consider a scenario some time around the turn of the century. British Gas, running out of natural gas reserves in the North and Irish Seas, is beginning to build its first synthetic natural gas plants which, when expanded into the envisaged 20-station network, will disgorge some 10 million tonnes of slag every year. To meet this new demand, coal output is doubled, and with the amount of colliery spoil arising from dumping. At around the same time, the CEGB will probably be building the first full scale coal-fired generating plant based on the pressurised fluidised bed technology which it is currently developing jointly with the National Coal Board. Barring an unexpected technical breakthrough, this single station alone — using large quantities of limestone to absorb sulphur oxide emissions — will add another 1-1.5 million tonnes of solid residues to the not inconsiderable pile created by the other energy industries.

The prospect, in land-scarce Britain, is utterly daunting, not least because official studies conducted since 1981 into spoil disposal methods such as backstowage into mines, remote disposal in worked-out quarries, and utilisation in road construction have offered little hope that an alternative to land dumping will be economically attractive. Equally, while the coal, gas and electricity utilities are all carrying out research programmes aimed at opening up new outlets for their coal production and utilisation residues none, so far, has given much encouragement that such outlets will swallow more than a very small proportion of the waste arisings.

The energy industries do not have a great deal of time to adjust to the fact that environmental upheaval on the scale which is likely to be required on present energy projections early in the 21st century will simply be unacceptable to the public. The sooner that planning to meet that eventuality begins — and that implies a reconstruction of Britain's energy policy around energy efficiency — the likelier it will be that disruption in energy supply can be avoided.

CHAPTER 5

ENERGY CONSER- VATION

ANDREW WARREN

IMITATION being the sincerest form of flattery, the international anti-nuclear movement should be suitably tickled by a couple of badges, samples of which are made freely available to all visitors to the plush London headquarters of the Electricity Council. The Council is the central body for all electricity distribution throughout England and Wales.

The first of these badges protrays a man dressed in a conventional bowler hat wearing an animal skin coat and shoes of obviously standard Briton wear. He looks both cold and fed-up. The second badge has (presumably the same) bowler-hatted gent rather gingerly toasting some presumed comestible over a fire using his umbrella as an improbable spear. The wording around the badges is distinctly similar — the first proclaims 'Ice age — no thanks', the second 'Dark ages — no thanks'; and both include the payoff line 'Atoms for Energy!'

Readers based anywhere in the western world will have recognised instantly what is being caricatured: it is that most familiar of all lapel badges and car stickers, the one with the beaming man-in-the-sun, surrounded by two phrases 'Nuclear Power' and 'No Thanks' translated into which ever language happens to be spoken locally.

One can fully understand the Electricity Council, and indeed the rest of the nuclear industry's frustration at what they undoubtedly perceive as a facile response to their endeavour to solve the energy crisis, and can

ATOMS FOR ENERGY! BUT IS THERE ANOTHER SOLUTION TO ENERGY
PROBLEMS ALONGSIDE CONTINUALLY EXPANDING THE SUPPLY?
(badges: The Electricity Council)

appreciate the temptation to seek to respond in kind. But those of us anxious to further the cause of the fifth fuel — of energy conservation or as it is now billed 'energy efficiency' — must respond with some irritation at the implication that **the** solution to our energy problems is to keep expanding the supply of energy full stop. And that anyone who dares question or suggest otherwise is some form of latter-day Luddite, determined to put the clock of progress back generations.

In the knowlege that clocks don't tend to work when turned backwards but rather stop altogether, we should indeed be foolish to let the demand management (another euphemism for energy conservation) alternative to supply investment be perceived in this way. But we have to face facts. One of the main reasons why energy conservation is not a sexy subject is that it still does retain just such unfortunate connotations of "doing without", of having to suffer to succeed.

Save It?

Yes, of course, we all know none suffer so much as those whose bank balances are burdened by having to meet unnecessarily high fuel bills, but reflect: when did we first hear about the energy crisis? In Britain you can date it exactly to October 1973 and the months immediately following the Yom Kippur War, when the three day week was introduced. It was a time, you may recall, of great suffering. Our television services were switched off early, public lighting displays were diminished, petrol coupons were issued.

Politicians went on TV (early in the evening before it was shut down) to worry us about the imminence of Armageddon. One senior minister earned some notoriety by advising us all to light only one room at a time in our homes, and clean our teeth in the dark (and got caught out by a smart photographer with the lights blazing in his home). A brand new Department of State was formed to look after the energy crisis.

Thus in the crucial intitial stages of awareness that energy was not an infinite commodity, conserving it came to be associated with emergencies, and rationing, and deprivation — and by implication subsequent advocacy of a deliberate reduction in its use, with entering a slippery slope towards a return to the Dark Ages in every sense.

When the October 1974 General Election was held in the U.K., the Labour Party won it using a propaganda poster which featured a flickering candle alone, a reminder of the suffering which the first burst of publicity for energy conservation had caused. Since then of course energy conservation promotion has become more sophisticated — of which more anon — with Britain leading the western world on how to set up public motivation, education and information policies on the topic.

When after strong pressure from President Jimmy Carter the International Energy Agency issued its energy conservation programme in 1979, they allocated areas of leadership to specific nations. The U.K.'s Department of Energy was placed in the driving seat to advise other nations how best to emulate their 'Save It' publicity campaign, probably the best remembered government-sponsored propaganda exercise in any field for many years. But even in itself the 'Save It' campaign was almost by definition negative, as it required people to do without something (a light, a heater, an open window) which, whether out of idleness or selfishness, they would in fact have preferred to continue using.

There was a graphic cartoon in the humorous magazine 'Punch' making just this point — a man sitting down, the curtains drawn, looking as miserable as sin. In the next door offices sat the same man in his shirt sleeves, with a fan blowing away, lights blazing, window open, with a happy smile on his face. The caption under the first office read 'Save It'; under the second, 'Sod It'.

Some of course did take to energy conservation instantly in a big way, and obtained a fair amount of publicity for it. But all too often it was merely an adjunct to a desire for an alternative lifestyle of back-to-nature self-sufficiency. It had an enormous appeal to a limited number of (admittedly articulate) middle class people. BBC TV centred one of their most popular comedy shows ever, "The Good Life" around it for the series featured a well-to-do middle class couple deciding to leave the rat race and live off the land. The land just happened to be their own suburban garden.

But such lifestyles would never, as they used to say in the Nixon White House "play in Peoria" (the British equivalent being Daventry or Lytham St. Annes). Conservation, it seemed, was for the brown rice and sandals brigade. It meant doing without all the useful household gadgets we've acquired. It meant standing in line in the rain for a dirty bus that never came. It meant, in short, reducing one's standard of living.

The rest of this chapter is devoted to ensuring that every reader acknowledges that such thinking is twaddle. Energy conservation (or energy efficiency, or demand management) makes sense because **it is a sound economic investment,** for householder, for business, for nation. It reduces the need to spend extra money and obtain extra land to produce further supplies of energy. The installation of energy saving artefacts creates an enormous number of jobs, and the successful functioning of energy saving measures in a factory or offices helps preserve existing jobs. And those who argue for it as one of the most cost effective investments anyone can make are not, repeat not, seeking to usher in the new Ice Age (SEE BOX 1).

Investing in Energy Conservation

First let us consider the case for energy conservation as a sound economic investment. Is there one? The answer is simple: in most circumstances, yes. Obviously some energy saving measures work better than others, and show a swifter rate of return than others. Equally some buildings begin with an in-built advantage over others, having been designed initially to conserve heat, both as a result of siting (in a sheltered situation, terraced, facing north-east), and also as a result of the initial inclusion of energy saving artifacts.

In Britain no new building of any type can be erected without satisfying at any rate the minimum energy conservation standards laid down in the Building Regulations. Most other European countries tend to have similar national codes; in the U.S.A., however, such measures are frequently only county or even municipally ordained.

Basically, a new home anywhere in Britain now will always have **some** loft insulation — around 100 cm — and **some** wall insulation. Floors will not have to be insulated (despite one-quarter of heat from such homes being lost through the ground). There is no requirement for even the most basic thermostatic control to be installed, let alone individual heating controls for each radiator. New offices and factories too will have some energy saving measures automatically built in, although usually to lower standards than homes (some form of heating controls are however, mandatory in commercial premises).

Of course many enlightened construction companies will build in far better energy saving measures than the bare minimum required by law — often because some enlightened prospective occupiers demand it. There is a growing tendency for the cost of occupying commercial premises to be expressed not just in terms of the basic rent and rates, but also including the annual running cost — a major component of which being the fuel bill. This is a very welcome sign, as it is only when building occupants stop accepting their fuel bills as merely an unavoidable overhead, and start perceiving them as a variable which they can reduce through sensible investment policy, that major inroads into energy waste can be made.

And there is certainly room for manoeuvre. The British Government's Energy Efficiency Office (staffed by civil servants within the Department of Energy) have publicly expressed a target of reducing the nation's

BOX 1.

Library Takes a Leaf out of the Energy Efficiency Book

Dramatic savings can accrue from a sound energy management policy. In one case, the Central Library in Newcastle upon Tyne, gas consumption was cut through a package of measures by **nearly 60%**. The payback period on the cost of the package was one year.

An energy audit in 1982 had revealed that the five-storey 9,000 sq metres 1960s concrete building was a comparatively high energy user. The survey also revealed that the existing boilers were unreliable and no longer conformed to gas safety standards.

In 1983–4 new boilers were fitted and a direct fired gas storage heater was installed to replace the calorifier system previously fed from the main boiler. External windows and doors were draught sealed. For maximum efficiency an energy management system was introduced with such features as sequence control of boiler plant, optimal stop/start cycles, duty cycling of air plants, maximum demand limiting, integral and proportional control and remote control via the telephone system.

But if all that sounds too complicated, bear in mind Glasgow City Council's Couper Institute. It was built in 1919 and has a large number of large vaulted halls and many side and anterooms. A 62% reduction in running costs was achieved through measures with a payback period of less than nine months. The method was simple — fitting low energy lighting.

waste by £7 billion each year. As at present national fuel bills are around £35 billion p.a., this argues that a 20% target for energy saving has been set. In fact, the head of their specialist Energy Technology Support Unit maintains publicly that 40% is equally feasible — and economic savings target on current bills. And the politicians' hyperbole maintains that by doing this, "Britian will be moved from the bottom to the top of the international energy conservation league in the lifetime of one Parliament," some five years at most! (SEE BOX 2).

One major barrier to energy saving investment, which causes particular concern in commercial premises, is the existence of short-term leasehold tenancies. An average homeowner moves every seven years; most conventional domestic energy saving measures will pay for their initial cost well within that time, and may well add to the potential re-sale value of the home, particularly if the purchaser is told about the likely lower running costs at the time of sale.

Office leases however are frequently granted for shorter periods, thus reducing the potential direct benefits to the occupier of installing too many energy saving measures. Equally, at the close of the lease, the asset-value of the premises — even if it has been upgraded by the tenants' wise investment in conservation — accrues to the landlord, who of course never pays the fuel bills directly himself. The same position obviously applies to those who rent their homes.

The tenant is frequently disinclined to install any more than, say, the most basic low-cost energy saving measures e.g. placing a jacket on an immersion heater, or some simple draftproofing. Measures which would in other circumstances, and considering the lifespan of the building, make sound sense, simply don't get installed.

This is a genuinely serious problem experienced throughout the world. As a result of such short-term thinking, far more fuel is used in each nation than is required by any objective rational standards. Further investment into new supply sources — oil wells, gas pipelines, power stations — are thereby encouraged, inevitably impinging upon some new part of the countryside or coastline.

Increasingly both nations and utilities are looking at the whole energy supply provision versus demand management equation in a harsher light. Is it possible that by, say underwriting the cost of installing insulation and heating controls into those buildings whose occupants (whether through ignorance or selfishness) can't or won't install the measures themselves, one can thereby reduce overall demand and obviate the need for further supply side investment?

BOX 2.

Alternative Energy Supply: Weird or Wonderfuel?

One way governments can conserve conventional fuel reserves is to encourage finding and use of alternative sources as a supplement or even substitute. Wind and wave both have possibilities. Does anyone dismissive of the potential of these alternatives as gimmicry have a solar powered calculator or watch? And one of the most valuable renewable energy sources is far from a gimmick — hydro-electric power.

Though most may not make significant contributions to any national power grid, alternative energy supplies are already significant in many local situations. The problem of its storage remains to be effectively solved but direct solar energy is invaluable in certain parts of the world for drying and preserving crops or fish. Some companies have recognised that direct solar power can generate markets and have developed domestic heating devices and one has even designed a solar-powered timber drying kiln for the small sawmill operator or furniture producer in the developing world.

A winner of a European Conservation award sponsored by Ford suggests that the most efficient solar energy converters and storers are trees. If properly managed woodland schemes were set up, modern high-technology plants could produce charcoal, a more efficient and cleaner solid fuel than coal, in quantities that could result in price parity with coal. If the trees were coppiced they could represent, without re-planting, a long term self-renewing source of energy.

But alternative supplies are already making an impact in developed markets. Though biogas digesters fermenting dung and crop residues are used in a large number of developing countries to supply methane-rich gas for cooking, lighting, running machines and generating electricity they do have economic equivalents in the Industrialised North. Biogas digesters are used on some farms and the gas generated on landfill sites by bacteria in the refuse they contain offers lower energy costs to certain nearby businesses. Landfill gas has been proven as an alternative fuel for industrial processes like brick manufacture and has been used to generate electricity and, with diesel, to run site vehicles.

The French government certainly has long thought so. All the activities undertaken by Agence Francaise Pour La Maitrise d'Energie, their very effective conservation promotion agency, are costed against the potential amount of oil saved. If saving the energy is cheaper for the French nation than purchasing it, then they are prepared to fund saving it — even if the immediate beneficiary is a private corporation or citizen. Similarly the U.S. government still echoes President Carter's view of energy conservation as the "moral equivalent of war". President Reagan's administration described conservation specifically in the National Energy Plan as a "significantly important energy resource" which is a "cost effective alternative to new supply development".

Many gas and electricity utilities, both privately and publicly owned, throughout the United States currently undertake detailed comparison exercises regarding capital resource allocation, and conclude that it is cheaper for them to reduce energy demand by installing conservation measures, than to invest in new supplies. Recognising the inevitable monopoly status of these utilities, each of the 50 states (except Nebraska) employ an official regulatory body, to help ensure that the fuel providers **do** undertake these equations which are in the stockholders', as well as the publics' interest.

Energy Efficiency means Job Opportunities

There is also a growing appreciation that sensible demand management (the other euphemism) policies can help to provide solutions to other major social problems. Throughout much of the developed world, particularly in inner cities and urban areas, are to be found many examples of rundown housing, warehouses and factories, put up years ago when fuel bills were peripheral to anyone's budget. Government everywhere acknowledge the need to try to improve these frequently dispiriting areas: some governments indeed have instituted or presided over programmes which try to ameliorate these problems.

This of course if just the time when energy saving is of vital importance: when a rundown building is being improved or retrofitted, it will improve its appearance, its effectiveness and its economics if simultaneously great care is taken to introduce conservation measures throughout.

The introduction of such measures will also help to confront another growing problem: the provision of worthwhile work for those with minimal skills or qualifications. Whilst the installation of energy saving artefacts (other than the most basic items like draughtstripping) is scarcely a Do-It-Yourself concept for other than great enthusiasts, prospective full time installers can be trained to carry out such work

BEFORE AND AFTER: SAVINGS ON THE FUEL BILL WERE MADE FOR
THEIR CLIENT WHEN ENERGY MANAGERS EMSTAR DECENTRALISED A 50
YEAR OLD MAIN BOILERHOUSE INTO SIX SEPARATE PLANT ROOMS
INSTALLING NEW GAS-FIRED BOILERS AND WATER HEATERS.
(photos: Emstar Ltd.)

with reasonable professionalism within a shortish period of time. It is also extremely labour intensive work. Indeed in many cases, it is the labour cost rather than the materials cost which forms the bulk of the initial 'capital' cost which prospective purchasers have to weigh against their eventual anticipated savings. Obviously this is less true regarding the sophisticated hi-tech side of energy efficiency: electronic energy management or lighting systems need both to be designed and installed by those well qualified to understand the system's intricacies.

But the fact remains that there is enormous potential for employment in this area, among the semi-skilled and unskilled. Hard figures to demonstrate the potential are not easy to come by: however, in 1983 the U.K. based Association for the Conservation of Energy published the findings of some detailed work undertaken on their behalf by the international consultancy Environmental Resources Ltd. This showed that up to 155,000 new jobs could be generated in this area in the U.K. alone over a 10 year period, with a programme far more 'profitable' than the British Government normally require for public sector captial investment. At present, less than 15,000 people are reckoned to be directly employed in the energy conservation field in the U.K., however generously defined.

The introduction of energy saving measures has also been welcomed in many factories and offices. This is not just by managers aware of the lower fuel costs and hence higher profits that can ensue. It is also welcomed by organised labour as a most unusual form of contemporary captial investment into a plant: one that does **not** require a direct reduction in the number of people employed on the premises in order to succeed. That has all too often been perceived as a *sine qua non* of other capital investment projects introduced by managements.

Fuelling Profits

For many businesses, fuel bills form a relatively small part of turnover, on average no more than 2 to 3%. As such, they appear on first sight to be of minor importance to senior management. However, a more accurate perception would be to compare the annual fuel bill with the operation's annual profit: in which case the percentage usually comes out a lot higher (SEE BOX 3).

When it is appreciated that any saving in the fuel bill goes straight into the bottom right hand corner of the balance sheet, the 'profit' side, companies tend to be far keener to take their energy bills seriously.

For energy conservation to work, it simply must not be seen as a negative concept. Suffering to save is seldom much fun. Nor must it be seen as a last-ditch attempt to stave off Armageddon (and its proponents as prophets of doom).

Energy conservation makes sense above all because it makes sound economic sense. That as a result a more pleasant world, with more jobs and more comfortable living conditions can accrue is just icing on the cake.

BOX 3.

Bussing in Lower Running Costs

Any measures cutting vehicle fleet fuel costs must be a welcome contribution to operators' overall cost control programmes. However the advantages of more fuel efficient vehicles are often discounted in the stop-start of heavy town traffic.

Systems are now available though which can considerably reduce bus fuel consumption through turning stop-start conditions to the operator's advantage. In one developed by Volvo an extra hydraulic pump/motor is fitted to the transmission system via a clutch. When the brakes are applied it acts as a pump, storing energy in hydraulic accumulators. When the bus accelerates it acts as a motor, driven by the pressurised hydraulic system, and assists the conventional diesel engine.

London Regional Transport (LRT) currently use 110 million litres of fuel per annum. Obviously even a single figure % reduction means a substantial cash sum saved. Though the system means the bus is heavier than one driven by conventional power alone, LRT's initial trials have shown City and Suburban operation fuel savings of 25–35%!

CHAPTER 6

AGRICULTURE AND ENVIRON- MENTAL HEALTH

TIMOTHY O'RIORDAN

AGRICULTURE HAS NEVER BEEN entirely environmentally benign though by and large, before the turn of this century, agriculture and environmental health were as one. But matters are much more serious today. In developed countries agriculture is an industry, a commercialised enterprise where profit making and maximising production are the dominant goals.

Since the Second World War agriculture has become the beneficiary of technological and genetic discoveries which have transformed its capacity to draw upon the natural provisions of the soil and of nutrient cycles. The productive vanguard of modern agriculture acts almost as if it were free of any natural environmental impediments. Wet soils are drained, unproductive soils are fertilised, insect and weed pests are eradicated and "unnecessary" features, often harbouring wildlife and delighting the eye, are removed or neglected. As we shall see, this technological escalator has raised agriculture into an extraordinarily costly activity where producers must constantly improve their performance to clear their debts. While small farmers are not so productive or demanding in natural systems, they are also suffering from the debt ripples which spread far and wide across the modern countryside, so are forced into management practices that undermine the nurturing capacity of their lands.

The Crisis in the Developing World

Much more serious, however, is the plight of the third world farmer. In the post colonial era a new form of colonisation has appeared. This has come through the take over of some of the best cultivable lands by multinational food conglomerates for the growing of commercial products such as fruit, coffee, tea, bananas and cattle. Many middle sized landowners or tenants are locked into cash crop, rather than indigenous food production, simply to pay off the debts owed to unscrupulous money lenders, seed merchants and corrupt landlords. The very poor, small scale farmers (many of whom are landless) are equally unable to clear their ever present borrowing requirements; many have to sell their "surplus" crop even before it is planted, while their children toil endlessly in the field or gathering fuelwood and fresh water. These very poor peasants have neither the resources, nor the skills or advice to improve their production. Agriculture is simply a matter of survival, and their environmental health is steadily diminishing.

The consequence of these pressures is desperate destruction of the regenerative capacity of soils, water and plant systems. Every year about 11 million hectares of arable land is lost due to erosion caused by surface sheetwash, gullying and the loss of the binding and stabilising properties of surface nutrients caused by overcropping. According to an authoritative study by Norman Myers, a distinguished environmental consultant, if trends continue, and there is unfortunately every indication that the problem will get worse, then the world shall lose over 275 million hectares. This is equivalent to one sixth of all existing arable lands, and ten times the total land area of the United Kingdom.

The UN Food and Agriculture Organisation and Environmental Programme regard soil erosion by far the most serious problem facing third world agriculture. As populations increase, more and more families are forced to cultivate marginal lands — steep slopes, deforested areas, dry grasslands, flood prone valleys, drought prone areas — which are entirely unsuited to the demands made upon them. Once a soil loses its fertility it is all but impossible to restore its environmental health. Vast tracts of the developing world are suffering from soil dessication — the drying out of savannah margins caused by overgrazing and toxification — the polluting of soil by salts drawn up from the subsoil by excessive irrigation and inappropriate cropping. Dessication, or desertification, claims over 24 million hectares of cultivable land annually, while toxification claims 50 million hectares each year. Straightforward soil erosion takes account of another 50 million hectares.

One of the great human and environmental tragedies of the modern era is the driving of the Third World poor into conditions of social and environmental degradation. Whole ecosystems are threatened, most notably the moist tropical forest. IUCN data would suggest that about 22 million hectares, or 6 percent of these forests are being destroyed or severely damaged every year due to logging agricultural incursion, fuelwood gathering and cattle ranching. This translates to a loss of some 42 hectares every minute. The loss of tropical hardwood forests leads to erosion, flooding, silting and the destruction of thousands of plant and insect species whose ecological and potential economic benefits are unknown. Worse still, if huge areas of the tropics become altered so that the moisture transfer from the tropics to the temperate regions is impaired, this could have very serious repercussions for crop production in North America, Europe and the Soviet Union. The trouble is that we really do not know what might happen if we continue to tamper with tropical ecosystems. Politicians prefer to do nothing until they are forced to look over the edge of an abyss. By then it will be far too late.

The Ethiopian calamity, the Sahelian crisis and the tropical forest destruction are all connected. Third World agriculture is destroying the capacity of the land to feed its people: drought, pestilence and earthquake merely worsen their plight. But natural hazard is not the main cause of their distress; the fundamental problem is that the economic and social structure of almost all third world countries drives the poor into extremes of environmental indebtedness, weakening even further their capacity for sustaining their future. This problem is worsened by the alarming growth of national indebtedness to major banks and donor nations, forcing these nations to produce even more cash crops to meet foreign loans.

International and development assistance, training, community self help, and conserving husbandry based on appropriate technology must all be harmonised within a programme of reforms over land ownership, money lending and commercial food production so that environmental health can be restored. This is a mighty tall order, but we are slowly facing up to the desperate urgency of the problem.

The rising economic and environmental costs of agriculture in the European Community and the U.K.

It is tempting to feel that this crisis of environmental destruction does not effect the U.K. After all does it not have one of the most efficient agricultural industries in the world? Productivity as narrowly measured in output per unit of input has been rising at over 2 percent for the past ten years, a far better record than in any other official economic activity, and output per employee has increased even faster. This is largely due to the growth in machinery and chemical use per unit of labour employed, though one must not forget the legacy of very considerable and successful research effort into plant and animal genetics and improved farm management techniques. That research effort is estimated to cost about £150 million annually. About half of this is provided by the agrochemical industry. The European Community is now self sufficient in all of the temperate goods, and only has to import about 25 percent of all foods and foodstuffs.

Because agricultural support has a social as well as an economic dimension, and because the small farm vote is politically very important in many European Member States, it is all but impossible for Agricultural Ministers to break the over production — over subsidisation cycle which so mightily affects the Common Agricultural Policy. Last year a start was made by imposing milk quotas on all Member States. But this was a crude measure which has turned out to be most unfair on some countries and, especially, certain farmers. A rigidly applied quota is no solution to the surplus problem, unless quotas can be traded and more imaginative measures are available to maintain farm incomes. Price manipulation is also no answer in itself: the agricultural industry cannot be so easily tuned.

The alarming truth is that European agriculture is so dependent on injections of money and resources such as chemicals, fossil fuel energy and machinery, that it cannot be slimmed down without causing enormous hardship for many rural communities. The total cost of support for agriculture in the U.K. is estimated in a report from the Comptroller and Auditor General to exceed £2,000 million in direct Treasury payments, even after refunds from the European Community have been received. Because the Community also levies an import tax on most agricultural products which would otherwise undercut the protected and subsidised community output, the time cost to the consumer, according to the Institute of Fiscal Studies, is nearer £4,000 million — or about £1,600 for every family in the nation. In the U.K., the typical upland farmer is subsidised to the tune of £8,000 annually while many of the more productive lowland farmers receive over £30,000 in grants and price supports.

Equally alarming is the growing indebtedness of British agriculture. In 1980/81 total farm borrowing was only £500 million: five years later it exceeded £5,500 million and is increasing at about £500 million annually. Many large farms now owe banks in excess of £500,000. In the past such vast borrowing could be justified on the grounds that subsidised agricultural income would remain relatively buoyant even during a period of economic recession. In addition, land prices had risen well beyond normal market value, largely because of price support, so landowners with sizeable holdings could carry an impressive collateral. At an average of £2,000 per acre, even a modest 300 acre property, with its buildings and machinery, would be worth £1 million.

These halcyon days are now over. Prices are bound to fall and land values have already begun to dip. In the past two years the British Government has reduced the money available for farm development grant by over £100 million with even more cuts likely. In narrow money terms, upland agriculture is not worth the amount of support it receives, but the social consequences, let alone the landscape and environmental effects, would be devastating if the small farmer was left to the harsh winds of market forces. Equally important, no politician is prepared to strip agriculture so that it is naked to "pure" market forces: under such conditions there would be no guarantee that British consumers would receive sufficient food at a quality and price that would be relied on.

So agriculture is really at the proverbial crossroads. It is too expensive to justify continuation of the massive investments in research and development expenditures that it has enjoyed in the past. It is too successful to need such injections of public support. And it is showing signs of suffering from the recent period of drawing from the environmental "banks" of soil fertility, the ability of wildlife to withstand damage or destruction of their habitats. This environmental "borrowing" simply has to stop. Not only is the nation's stock of wild plants and animals threatened, but thoughtless misuse of agricultural ecosystems will inevitably result in additional costs — of restoration or remedying damage — which are proving both unnecessary and intolerable. Let us look at the environmental costs of modern agriculture in the U.K.

Soil erosion. For a long time it has been widely believed that Britain does not suffer from the scale of soil erosion that affects the U.S. and the Third World. British agriculture was regarded as conserving and even nurturing for soil health. Alas, this is no longer the case. Surveys concluded by the Soil Survey of England and Wales since 1971 show that surface and especially rill erosion (caused by rainwater exploiting breaks of slope) has increased dramatically. Whereas typical soil loss under a mature woodland would be of the order of 0.25 tonnes per hectare, under light soils erosion rates can exceed 40 tonnes per hectare. This rate of loss is sufficient to destroy the fertile top layer of soil in 25-40 years. The resulting siltation can clog streams and impoverish adjacent fields. The main causes are the rapid spread of winter cereal production, ploughing down the slope and rainfall patterns where sudden bursts fall on already saturated soils.

Nitrates. Nitrates are associated both with inorganic fertiliser, application and slurry discharges. Since 1960 the potassium element in fertiliser use has remained almost stable, at around 190,000 kg annually, the phosphorus component has increased slightly to 400,000 kg but the nitrate constituent has grown from 400,000 kg to nearly 1.5 million kg. Currently there is a lot of disagreement amongst scientists as to the ultimate effect of nitrates on human health. There are those who argue that nitrates carried into the atmosphere through wind erosion of light, fertilised soils, add to the nitrification, and hence acidity of rainfall. Others believe that nitrates from overfertilised fields pass into the groundwater to pose a threat to young babies drinking the contaminated water. There is widespread agreement that animal slurry, a feature of the trend toward more intensive livestock production, is polluting lakes and rivers with excessive doses of nutrients. These encourage the growth of water weeds and algae. Algae in particular, destroys healthy aquatic ecosystems, choking many interesting water plants and associated insect life.

In 1979 the Royal Commission on Environmental Pollution examined the possible public health effects of nitrates. Although nitrates are non toxic when ingested in food or in water, they are partially converted to nitrites which can affect blood oxygen levels. The symptom is known as the "blue baby" syndrome, because very young infants are particularly susceptible to methaemoglobinaemia. The World Health Organisation has adopted a recommended limit of 50 milligrammes (mg) of nitrate per litre as an acceptable concentration, but its experts group is well aware that standards of hygiene and the presence of bacteria vary enormously, so the 50 mg level is really only a guide.

The Royal Commission also examined the evidence of a possible link between nitrates, nitrogen compounds in food, body acids and cancer. Some of the nitrate compounds in food are deliberately added in the form of preservatives, which also deepen the red colour of uncooked meat. The resulting N-nitroso compounds are known to cause gastric cancer in experimental animals. There is also some evidence of a correlation between high nitrate levels in drinking water and elevated incidence of gastric cancer in human beings, but casual linkage is difficult to prove. Although the Royal Commission was unwilling to recommend any lowering of the WHO level it pointed to the inconsistency of policy and advice regarding the availability of bottled water where nitrate levels in drinking water consistently exceeded 50 mg per litre. In July 1985 the Government implemented the European Community Directive on Drinking Water. This sets a limit of 50 mg per litre for nitrate concentrations, but the Government has decided to issue derogations (legal allowance) of 42 of the 52 supplies with nitrate concentrations above 50 mg per litre. However, the Directive requires the derogations are not permissible where there is a public health hazard, or where nitrate concentrations do not result from "the nature and structure of the ground". Since nitrate levels in U.K. groundwater are due to grassland conversion and fertilisation, and since scientific dispute over the nitrate-cancer link is by no means concluded, there is still scope for community litigation against the British decision.

BOX 1

Natural Recruits to Pest Control

There are many instances of crops devastated by burgeoning pest populations because non-selective sprays have wiped out their controlling predators. Predators are a significant factor in controlling population and in certain circumstances they can be turned directly to the growers' advantage.

Pests of such diverse crops as sugarcane, pasture grasses, vegetables and even coconuts have all been successfully countered through artificially introducing the appropriate predators, a measure known as **Biological Pest Control**. The need for environmentally sensitive chemicals is reduced or eliminated.

The technique is no great new initiative having been around for some time. As long ago as the late 19th Century the cottony-cushion scale, a pest in the Citrus groves of Southern California, was virtually eliminated by an introduced Australian Ladybird.

In its turn Australia itself provides perhaps the most renowned example of successful biological pest control. The prickly pear cactus is native to North and South America. It was exported around the world partly due to its security value as a formidable hedging material. By 1880 one species taken to Australia was out of control and had reached pest proportions. It rapidly spread in Queensland and New South Wales, occupying 5 million hectares in 1900 and a vast 30 million by 1925. Much of the area was covered so densely with cacti it was impossible to walk through.

Poisoning was no answer for this cost many times the value of the grazing land infested. Farms and homesteads were simply abandoned in the face of the spreading cactus.

Until the 1920's efforts to find a natural control amongst the insects living on the prickly pear in its home range only met with limited success. Then an Argentinian moth, rather appropriately named *Cactoblastis cactorum*, was found whose larvae significantly damaged the cactus by burrowing into its leaf pads to feed, introducing bacterial and fungal infections on the way. Introducing the moth to Australia had a devastating effect on the prickly pear population. By 1940 only scattered plants remained, controlled by the moth.

There again, if the situation had been managed properly in the first place maybe the prickly pear would not have been taken to Australia!

Pesticides. The European Community Directive also sets a limit of 0.1 microgramme (ug) per litre for individual chemical formulations, and 0.5 ug per litre for total pesticide concentrations in drinking water. In many British water supplies, herbicide concentrations alone exceed these levels. It would cost many millions of pounds to replace the traditional sand filters with activated carbon filters to remove these traces of potentially toxic compounds. The British, however, believe the Community's standards are far too high and have refused to implement the Directive in this regard.

As in the case with fertilisers, pesticide and herbicide applications have increased dramatically since 1960. Nowadays, pesticide sales exceed £300 million annually of which nearly three fifths is spent by agriculture. In 1982 herbicides accounted for 30% of the variable costs of cereal production. A recent official survey revealed that since 1974, field application of pesticides generally has increased eleven times in the U.K. The rise in agrochemical usage is due to a combination of factors — new varieties that are very dependent on chemical protection, disease resistance to established chemicals, the clamour for more pest-specific formulations so as to protect environmentally friendly birds, insects and plants (SEE BOX 1), the requirement by supermarket chains for blemish-free produce, and the relatively low cost of application compared to the possible losses of income should a crop be unsuitable for marketing. It is not unusual for modern farmers to spray a crop 5-8 times in a growing season.

The Royal Commission was concerned at the apparent cavalier use of pesticides and recommended that usage should be reduced so as to be consistent with efficient food production. The Commission, however, saw no reason to become alarmed about possible danger to public health because of pesticide traces in food. It was far more worried about the dependence which farmers had for chemicals, and the increase in insects and fungi which had become resistant to chemicals.

Wildlife had been more seriously affected by pesticides, and more latterly herbicides. In the 1960s scientific research showed that the breeding failure in many birds of prey (notably the osprey, falcon and eagle) was due to the effects of spraying organochlorides, of which DDT and dieldrin were the most notorious examples. These chemicals are soluble in fat and very persistent. So they build up through the food chain to reach considerable concentrations in the fatty tissues of flesh-eating birds and animals. For example, the spectacular crash in the U.K. peregrine falcon population was caused largely by the falcons eating pigeon which in turn had fed on seeds dressed with aldrin or dieldrin. Since 1970 most of these particularly persistent chemicals have been phased out, though environmental groups remain concerned that they are still on sale and their actual use is unmonitored.

More of concern today is the unsystematic effects of pesticides and herbicides on the soil organisms and insect life which would otherwise be natural predators to pests and parasites. Research by Dr. Dick Potts of the Game Conservancy has shown that young partridge chicks are being slowly starved due to lack of insects on which they would normally feed. Coupled with recent severe winters, this has had a devastating effect on wild partridge populations. Dr. Potts' work has caused many farmers not to spray their field margins. The result has been a gratifying rise in partridge populations together with an increase in hedge and field side flowers. The loss of crop production is insignificant compared to the gain in wildlife.

Agriculture, Wildlife and the Landscape

In recent years there has been an enormous amount of adverse publicity targeted at the agricultural community over the destruction of landscape features and wildlife habitats alleged to be the result of intensive and thoughtless agricultural production. The farming lobby responded by claiming that it does care about the environment, and that more land is lost to roads, housing and industrial development than as a consequence of modern farming practice. But research by Professor Robin Best of Wye College has shown that the loss of agricultural land due to development is relatively small and declining — at round about 1,200 hectares per year. In any case, removal of wildlife habitats and landscape features to development is less likely if proper planning procedures are followed.

Of far greater significance is the loss of wildlife habitat and characteristic landscapes due to the intensification and mechanisation of agriculture since 1960. Until recently, these changes were not notified in advance to planning authorities or conservation interests, and even today, formal warning is only required for less than 10% of the countryside. A report issued by the Nature Conservancy Council last year makes sombre reading. The report observed that "all main types of ecosystem have suffered appreciable loss, but for some, the scale and rate have been catastrophic". In presenting the study of the Nature Conservancy Council (NCC) Chairman, Mr. William Wilkinson, observed that "Conservationists are regularly pressed to compromise. The answer in most cases must be no". The gloomy position is one of a depleted natural heritage which may prove almost impossible to restore.

Perhaps even worse, is the sad record of agriculturally induced damage to protected sites of special scientific interest (SSSI), the jewels in the NCC's conservation crown. SSSIs are no ordinary areas: they are selected for their representativeness, diversity and scarcity value as well as being of immense scientific, educational and landscape value. Yet since 1981, when SSSIs were legally protected against abuse, over 300 SSSIs have been damaged, 150 alone between April 1983 and March 1984. In many cases this was due to wanton, but legal, destruction by an irate landowner. Sadly, however, other sites have been lost because the NCC and the landowner could not agree on an appropriate management agreement or terms of compensation. Happily the picture is a little more rosy today. The NCC has additional money and manpower to safeguard SSSIs, but the damage and neglect is quite serious and the cost of restoration and, especially, management, quite formidable.

Equally annoying to the conservation minded is the loss of many features that have made British rural landscapes so distinctive and cherished. The decline or removal of the hedgerow, the hedgerow tree and the free standing amenity hardwoods of oak, beech and ash are particularly grieved, though in the case of elm, most of the losses have been due to disease. Many wild moorlands have been tamed by under-drainage and reseeding with hardy fescue grasses, while too many wetlands have been drained for conversion to arable. These losses have been compounded by the neglect or removal of copses, spinneys and other small broadleaved woodlands.

Towards an Environmentally Friendly Agriculture

The British love their countryside. For generations, poets, novelists, philosophers and millions of ordinary people have sung the praises of the great landscapes of the nation. Over three quarters of British society regularly visit the countryside every year, and membership of conservation and amenity organisations exceeds 3 million and continues to grow. Birdwatching, fishing, strolling down byways and picnicing in beauty spots are long cherished traditions. The British will not tolerate the loss of their natural and cultural heritage. The impact of agriculture and forestry on the land is now a major political issue and recently all political parties have struggled to jump onto the "green" bandwagon.

At the heart of this green resurgence is a need for a comprehensive policy towards the care of the land. How might this policy look?

Firstly, we must capitalise on the achievements of agriculture. There is no longer any need to convert every potentially productive acre to the highest yielding crop: we neither require the produce, nor can we afford it. It is nonsense to talk of exporting surplusses to the starving Third World for subsidised external food aid acts only as a short term palliative. To rely on aid as a permanent solution would be disastrous

NEW SPRAYING TECHNOLOGIES OFFER COST EFFECTIVE WAYS TO
REDUCE POLLUTION: ICI'S ELECTRODYNE SPRAYER PRODUCES AN
ELECTRICALLY CHARGED MIST OF DROPLETS THAT "STICK" TO CROPS

AND USE LESS CHEMICAL AND LESS WATER, A FEATURE THAT
MAKES IT ATTRACTIVE IN ARID REGIONS.
(Photos: ICI Plant Protection Division)

for Third World farmers, and would undermine their capacity to produce sufficient food given suitable advice, technology and price incentives and appropriate developmental assistance.

So we should be aiming at a lower cost agriculture, an agriculture that is less demanding on soil structure and fertility, wildlife diversity and the cleansing properties of water. This does not mean to suggest that agriculture should revert to a pre-war state. On the contrary, the very best brains should be put to work to devise an ultra-modern agriculture that is both environmentally friendly and productive.

This means creating plant strains that require less artificial fertiliser, new fertiliser products that act directly at the root zones, advanced tillage techniques that are kinder to the soil and pest control strategies that rely on biological processes more than unnatural chemicals. Already there are spraying technologies which are much more environmentally benign but which should be improved further. The bio-engineering industry is poised to produce biocides which are highly selective in individual species with few ecological side effects. These developments have to be encouraged. It is heartening to report that both the agrochemical industry and the main research councils are actively pursuing research and development into a whole host of more environmentally tolerant products and practices (SEE BOX 2).

Second, we must change the levers of influence on agricultural investment away from intensification and wasteful compensatory payments in lieu of not doing something that would be environmentally demanding towards a "whole farm" approach for integrating conservation measures within sustaining agriculture. Conservation measures should not be confined to the field margins and tree-planting — the cosmic face of a guilty agricultural conscience. The new farm conservation programmes should address the thoughtful care of established landscape and habitat features, based on the best practical advice, the provision of public access to a well managed farm, and investment in creative conservation, the creation of new habitats and landscapes for our great grandchildren to enjoy.

It is encouraging to report that the European Commission is very much aware of the need to devise policies and financial inducements to promote this new "whole farm" image. In a recently published consultative document, the agricultural directorate spoke clearly of the need to link agriculture to environmental requirements and social wellbeing. The British Government has just announced a new scheme of agricultural improvement grants to encourage farmers to interlock conservation within agricultural development.

BOX 2

Land of Opportunity in Environmentally Healthier Techniques

Environmentally more benign farming techniques like low volume sprayers and agrobiological sprays, besides offering advantages to growers, also present new opportunities to equipment manufacturers and materials suppliers.

The laboratory and back garden method of seeding called "Fluid Sowing" may represent another such opportunity. With fluid sowing seeds are planted in a jelly envelope a little like wallpaper paste. The advantage is that no matter what the soil conditions the gel holds water crucial for germination around the seeds.

It holds commercial attractions as it could significantly reduce costs: less seed is needed for the same yields and the seed need not be expensively clay-coated to a uniform size as required by some handling equipment. At the germination stage less chemicals are required as they can be placed where they are wanted — in the gel around each seed — instead of being conventionally, wastefully and expensively broadcast.

Third, we must ensure that our truly cherished habitats and landscapes are guaranteed to be protected and properly managed. This means a system of advance notification of any possible alterations and the availability of sufficient resources either for the conservation minded to acquire such sites or for well-advised landowners to manage these areas in accord with agreed principles. Already a good, if belated, start has been made for SSSIs and national nature reserves. The Countryside Commission has just announced an important new programme for highlighting the national importance of National Parks. And the Ministry of Agriculture is about to designate a small number of Environmental Sensitive Areas (ESAs) where it will provide special payments to farmers to retain traditional forms of management. In the first instance, these areas are most likely to be marshes, moorlands and possibly some woodlands. The idea is still experimental, but hopefully the ESA will prove to be the forerunner of a shining new Common Agricultural Policy.

Fourth, we must take care to protect the livelihood of small and marginal farmers who not only can do so much care for the land, which, without them, would otherwise be neglected or expensively maintained by conservation interests, but who provide such an important mainstay for the remoter rural communities. The story of British agriculture since the war has also been one of labour shedding and inadvertent discrimination against part time farmer and small holder. This woeful imbalance of official support favouring the big and the wealthy at the expense of the small and the vulnerable must be redressed. We must co-ordinate economic policy with agricultural and environmental strategies. Direct income support, assistance for off-farm employment opportunities, encouragement of community enterprise schemes, the streamlining of all the red tape so that financial support, proper advice and training and the achievements of experiments must all be fitted together to make the landscape and the people who create and maintain it more lively and caring.

The vehicle for this rather utopian vision is the concept of integrated rural development. So far this has suffered from lack of political support and the myopic determination of public agencies to confine themselves to their policy playpens. Agriculture, forestry, education, community development, environmental enhancement, individual enterprise, tourism and the arts cannot remain isolated from each other, jealously demarcated by self-serving interests. If the countryside is to prosper and to continue to provide inspiration, it must be managed as a totality, a bundle of opportunities and challenges. In the mid 18th century the agricultural revolution paved the way to a new industrial Britain. In the late 20th century, another agricultural revolution could equally spark off a post-industrial renaissance, not just in the countryside but throughout the national economy.

CHAPTER 7

FINANCE
AND
DEVELOP-
MENT

I T IS DIFFICULT
ENOUGH for any person
(educated or not) to
understand how, say, the rate
support system works in Britain,
the welfare state or how the money
from the European Commission
flows back and forth across
national boundaries. It is nigh on
impossible to understand how
international finance works. We
hear of the debt crisis; one minute
it is solved then it is not; there is a
run on the dollar; the World Bank
gets another 20 billion to spend in
the Third World and so on and so
on. The pages of the financial
press read like a multi-million
dollar roller coaster. Does this all
connect? Does someone know how
it works? What does it mean to
you and me and the world out
there? And why does it concern
the environment?

Simple answers have a habit of being misleading but . . .

One half of the world is rich in comparison to the other half. In fact
the rich "half" is not a half at all. One quarter of the world's population
living in the industrialised North earn 80% of the Gross Global Product
or GGP (SEE BOX 1.). Nearly one billion of the world's population live in
absolute poverty and some 450 million of these are starving or
malnourished.

BOX 1.

Rich Man, Poor Man

"Absolute poverty" is hard to comprehend for anyone living in the world's developed North. There are some very poor people though, where there is resort to some form of welfare, chances are better than for the poor of the South. These people live in absolute poverty, which has been described by a former President of the World Bank as a "condition of life so characterised by malnutrition, illiteracy, disease, high infant mortality and low life expectancy as to be beneath any reasonable definition of human decency". And these poor are getting poorer on the global scale. Per Capita incomes (derived by dividing the annual flow of money in a country's economy by the population) have fallen dramatically in parts of Latin America and Africa. Effectively 40 people in many of these countries have to live on what is the per capita income of just one person in the richer North. And the rich are getting richer . . .

Per capita income, though, is quite different from any external debt which is the amount of money a government owes to creditors abroad. The heaviest debt burdens are carried by the countries classed as "newly" rich, Brazil being the biggest debtor in the world and owing $90 million in 1980.

This debt burden means that the country has interest to pay — in formidable amounts. The total debt of developing countries in 1983 was about $800 billion (long and short term) and it now amounts to about one and a half times their annual export earnings. Half this debt is owed to private financiers (banks such as the National Westminster or Chase Manhattan Bank), the rest to governments or governmental institutions. Every year the interest and service payments on the debt is over $100 billion (1983 — $20 billion 1973). In some cases this interest eats up one third to one half of a country's annual export earnings. The full force of the position comes to light when you realize that in 1983 developing countries experienced a negative net flow of funds into their economies — that is to say gross borrowing minus debt servicing payments — amounted to $11 billion. They got a lot poorer. They paid us more than we traded to them.

Where does this leave charitable aid (Mr Geldoff or Oxfam), official government aid (from Britain, France or wherever), or multilateral aid from the United Nations or the World Bank?

The Aid Money Supply

All three categories — private flows, government to government flows and multilateral (or many government) are the reverse to interest payments and debt repayments. In total they amount to some $30 billion a year. This money goes to finance that development. But it is not as simple as that. Some goes straight to the poor — in the form of projects at a village at community level (private charitable flows). Some goes to governments for development, including village and community schemes, as a direct grant. Some goes via the United Nations who in turn pass it on to governments for development projects. Then there is money paid to the multilateral development banks — as subscribed capital — which in turn is lent at a rate of interest. These banks also raise money on the world's money markets in much the same way as governments do with bonds. All this is lent to those governments in need.

There are four multilateral development banks or MDBs: the World Bank, Inter-American Development Bank (IDB), Asian Development Bank and African Development Bank. In 1984 these four institutions lent over $22 billion for development projects in the Third World. The lending activities for these banks dwarf the activities of all other governmental and international agencies operating in the developing world. The World Bank, HQ in Washington DC, alone accounts for three quarters of the total lending of the four MDBs and is by far the most powerful and influential.

It is also relevant to mention the International Monetary Fund (IMF) when discussing the MDBs. The IMF is not an aid agency, but rather the linchpin, along with the World Bank with which it works in tandem, of the entire international financial system. When a country is literally on the verge of going bankrupt through no longer having enough foreign exchange to pay for imports and/or the interest on its existing foreign debt the IMF will give emergency loans as the international lender of last recourse. The conditions the IMF and World Bank demand of a country to get it back on its feet are draconian, but Third World countries have little choice. These conditions almost inevitably require that a country reduce its public services and increase agricultural export production.

In summary there are rich, not so rich and poor countries giving or receiving grants, loans, concessionary loans or special drawing facilities. And on top there is private money and trade flowing around to make the story almost complete.

But it does not end there for in addition there are currencies — many of them — and interest rates. Essentially there are currencies tied to the dollar, those to the rouble, those linked together in Europe (in the so called snake or European Monetary System) and the rest. Interest rates go up and down depending on the domestic position of countries, leading to complex problems of debt repayment and debt scheduling and currency values. Countries heavily in debt have weak currencies and often as not rampant inflation. Bolivia, for example, has an inflation rate of about 100% per day or 2,400% per annum (compared with Britain's 5 - 6% yearly). All in all we owe our lives to the economists.

That would be fine if the economists were actually in control and accountable to us. They are not. Yet the decisions they make, and in turn the decisions the market place makes for them on supply and demand determine the outcome of peoples' lives. For instance, if you were running a country in debt you might decide to work hard to pay the debt off and become self reliant. To do this you might decide to grow coffee, or peanuts or carnations for export. To do that needs land. So land is obtained and you begin exporting well. But others have the same idea and in any case the market depends on someone being rich enough to buy the coffee. At this point competition sets in and everyone is trying to grow export commodities and the price begins to fall as shown by Tanzania's sisal: 17,25 tonnes were needed to buy a tractor in 1965 but in 1974 57% more had to be sold. You end up having to run ever faster to keep up in a world where your commodity prices are controlled by the rich in the North who lent the money to start growing them in the first place.

The multi-lateral development banks and IMF are quasi-sovereign, autonomous international entities. They are governed by Boards of Executive Directors which must approve every loan and every significant change of policy and proceedure. The Directors represent the member nations, in the case of the World Bank 148 different countries, but their voting power is proportional to the financial contributions of their countries. In the World Bank, for instance five of the twenty one Directors are appointed by the five countries who contribute most to the Bank.

The U.S. Director of the World Bank has about 20% of the total voting power, far more than any other nation. The U.K., Federal Republic of Germany, France and Japan have the other four 'appointed' directors, each with between five and six per cent of the voting power. The other 16 Directors are 'elected' by several countries to represent them as a group. But a number of these Directors also come from developed countries and their voting influence is far greater than any of the Third World Countries' elected Director.

The MDBs are required by their charters to lend mostly for specific projects. The environmental problems and adverse effects that result from such projects are particularly severe because of their large scale, capital intensive nature. More than half the lending goes for mammoth agricultural, hydroelectric and water management schemes involving major and often disastrous impacts on wildlife, destruction of tropical forests and irreplaceable habitats and misuse of toxic pesticide and agrochemicals on a massive scale.

Moreover, the projects and policies of the MDBs have a much greater impact on the ecological stability and environmental future of the Third World than even the huge dollar amounts of their annual loans would indicate. In general, one MDB dollar attracts two to three dollars in matching funds from national sources. But the MDBs retain the 'lead' on almost all projects that they help finance, which means that they have the final say in the design and planning of such projects, and, indeed in the kinds of development projects that Third World governments promote.

Thus it is not surprising that many countries modify their national development plans in response to the 'suggestions' and pressures of the

MDBs. An important element in this policy influence is the 'policy and sector' work of the Banks, the general policy and strategy documents that the MDBs prepare to help identify and analyse priorities in lending. The influence of the World Bank is particularly important in this regard, and the combination of World Bank policy documents and high level dialogues with host country officials has a profound effect.

A final element in the tremendous power and leverage of the MDBs lies in the fact that no Third World country can obtain commercial loans from private international banks unless it has the 'stamp of approval' of the MDBs, starting with the World Bank. Private international banks such as Chase Manhattan will not lend to countries on the economic ropes unless they have complied with IMF/World Bank conditions for a bailout loan. Indeed private banks will only participate in financing specific development projects like roads or dams if an MDB takes part in the financing and leads the project planning.

Finance and Environmental Threat

The MDBs **could** ensure through their leverage and influence that the environment is conserved rather than destroyed but much of what they do is accelerating ecological devastation. Ironically, the multilateral banks all have made formal declarations of environmental policy which, if realistically implemented, would allow them to play a positive role in conserving the world environment. If, for instance, any campaign on conserving the tropical rainforests is to succeed it must dramatically change the policies and practices of the MDBs and the IMF.

The single gravest global threat posed to wildlife by the multilateral finance system is probably the contribution it makes to accelerating deforestation of the tropics. The MDBs finance projects like cattle ranches, jungle colonisation schemes, hydroelectric dams and irrigation schemes on a massive scale which directly contribute to deforestation and destruction of habitats. Moreover they are helping to promote implementing general agricultural policies that are capital rather then labour intensive. These displace Third world rural farmers and the poor from better lands suitable for agriculture into agriculturally marginal wildlife habitat areas such as tropical moist forests.

Over the last 20 years the MDBs have financed cattle projects on a large scale, especially in Central and South America. These projects have contributed directly and indirectly to accelerating deforestation and wildlife extinction. Directly it is by converting huge areas of pristine forest to pasture, indirectly through ranches replacing smaller subsistence farming on soils suited for perennial agriculture, prompting the migration of the uprooted rural population to marginal forest areas.

Ironically even the small farm plots in cleared forest areas are converted to pasture after two or three years because of declining yields on the poor soils.

According to one estimate, the total investments (including government matching funds) that World Bank and IDB projects channelled into livestock projects during 1970–77 alone was around $5 - 7 billion ($10 - 14 billion 1984 dollars). No single commodity in the Third World has ever received such extraordinary outside support as South American livestock. But in spite of the overwhelming evidence of the environmental unsoundness and economic wastefulness of cattle projects, especially in Latin America, the development banks are continuing to finance them on a substantial scale.

The environmental and economic justification for the forest colonisation projects financed by the MDBs are even more dubious. The major ecological factor in the abysmal performance of these schemes is the generally poor quality of the soils in tropical moist forests. Perhaps 90% of tropical moist forest soils are completely unsuited for any kind of annual agriculture. The only people that have evolved sustainable agro-ecosystems in these areas are the indigenous and tribal peoples that inhabit many of the still intact rainforests. Regrettably the MDBs are doing little to investigate, preserve and utilise this knowledge and much through ill-conceived agricultural projects to accelerate its decline. In the words of one anthropologist:

With the extinction of each indigenous group, the world loses millenia of accummulated knowledge about life in, and adaptation to tropical ecosystems. This priceless information is forfeited with hardly a blink of the eye: the march of development cannot wait long enough to find out what it is destroying.

Since 1960, six percent of IDB lending has gone for agricultural settlement schemes in tropical forest regions. The World Bank and IDB are currently implementing a number of recently approved settlement schemes in tropical rainforest areas with generally poor soils. In 1982 the World Bank approved a $42.7 million loan (total project cost: $122.9 million) to Brazil for rural development and agricultural settlement in Maranhao state in the northeast Amazon. This project risks worsening the deforestation and ecological destruction caused by a previous partly failed project financed by the bank in the same region, the Alto Turi Settlement Project. The IDB approved two loans totalling 46 million in 1982 for a roadbuilding and agricultural settlement project in the Pichis Valley in the Peruvian Amazon. The soils in this region are so bad that the World Bank itself refused to fund any development in the area.

Financing Disaster

The MDBs are embroiled in a controversy concerning their ongoing financing of two mammoth settlement programmes in Indonesia and Brazil that have been categorised as ecological debacles. Arguably these MDB tropical forest settlement projects are doing more to exterminate rare and unknown animals and plants than any other activity on earth. The World Bank and Asian Development Bank are providing over one billion dollars in loans to help finance the Indonesian transmigration programme. The goal is to move millions of people from the densely populated inner islands, mainly Java, to the still forested outer islands such as Borneo, Irian Jaya and Sumatra. The volcanic soils of Java are extremely fertile whereas the outer islands have the extremely poor soils unsuited for small farmer annual cropping typical of tropical moist forests. The adverse environmental impact of transmigration of settlers onto these poor soils have been enormous, including large scale deforestation, species extinction, erosion and flooding. Although the World Bank has justified its role by claiming that it is trying to make transmigration environmentally sounder, the programme was ecologically disastrous in its very conception.

Recently the World Bank's largest and most disastrous involvement in forest colonisation in the tropics is its financing of the Brazil Northwest Development Programme (Polonoroeste) for which the Bank has approved six loans since 1981 totaling $443.4 million. The overall cost of the Amazon colonisation, settlement consolidation and road construction scheme approaches $1.6 billion.

The Bank's Polonoroeste investment is essentially a highway project covering a forested area three quarters the size of France. It involves the paving of a 1,500 kilometer highway through the heart of the southwestern Amazon basin and construction for feeder and access roads and 39 rural settlements to attract tens of thousands of settlers. Over 8,000 Amerindians belonging to about 34 tribal groups are thought to live in the area, though since some parts of the Polonoroeste region are so remote there may be at least two or more tribes who have had no contact with the outside world.

What is happening in the Polonoroeste region is an ecological, human and economic disaster of tremendous dimensions. The rate of deforestation in the programme area is the highest in the Brazilian Amazon and still increasing. Countless species of animals and plants, many never identified or studied, are being exterminated. If present trends continue the entire Brazilian state of Rondonia, an area the size of Great Britain, will be deforested by 1990. The public health situation is a tragedy. The incidence of malaria is close to 100% in some areas.

Some Indian tribes are menaced with extermination from measles and influenza epidemics and infant mortality rates of 25 and 50 per cent have been reported in two recently contacted tribes.

Rather than being 'consolidated', as was the intention of the Bank, settlers are abandoning their cleared land since it cannot support annual cropping. In many instances they are selling it to larger landowners for cattle ranching, a use which numerous past experiences in the Amazon have shown will also be unsuitable.

An article in the journal **Foreign Affairs** describes the scenes of massive ecological devastation in the Indonesian Transmigration and Polonoroeste projects:

Visiting such areas is hard to view without emotion, the miles of devastated trees, of felled, broken and burned trunks, of branches, mud, and bark crisscrossed with tractor trails — especially when one realizes that in most cases nothing of comparable value will grow again on the area. Such sights are reminiscent of photographs of Hiroshima, and Brazil and Indonesia might be regarded as waging the equivalent of thermonuclear war upon their territories.

Investments a washout?

The World Bank financed nearly $6 billion worth of hydro projects in the period 1980–82 and provided nearly $1 billion for irrigation and drainage in 1982 alone. But MDB water management projects are also disrupting wildlife habitats and causing large scale ecological destruction. The huge environmental problems caused by hydro electric and irrigation projects can only be partially mitigated (SEE BOX 2). Such impacts include:

— the forced displacement of a large number of people through flooding, including vulnerable indigenous tribes;

— the inundation of tropical forests, of great biological and scientific significance;

— the salination and water-logging of irrigated lands;

— the siltation and sedimentation of reservoirs and channels through deforestation of adjacent watersheds; and,

— the spread of water-borne diseases, including malaria, schistosomiasis and onchocerciases (river blindness).

BOX 2.

Dam Problems

Egypt's Aswan Dam was supposed to provide much needed hydroelectric power, which it did. What it was not supposed to do was silt up. In turn this silt held back in Lake Nasser used to fertilise fields and fisheries downsteam as well as provide brickmakers with their raw materials. Environmental factors were not fully considered during planning. Fertiliser imports were forced up and fisheries and brick manufacturers' interests were affected. On top of that irrigation problems affected agricultural production still further and people living alongside the new lake and irrigation canals suffered in an epidemic of schistosomiasis, a water-based parasitic disease.

There are both direct and indirect human costs to ill-considered projects and their accompanying financial packages. The direct cost is measured in suffering through ill-health, dispossession and poverty, disaster in supporting croplands and starvation. The indirect costs are harder to define because we do not know what is being lost. The incredible diversity of the tropical rainforests, for instance, could conceal a multitude of invaluable products, one study suggesting there are more than 1,000 plants with economic potential in the Amazon forest alone. Products derived from one tropical rainforest plant, the Rosy Periwinkle, have dramatically improved the chances of survival of children with leukaemia and sufferers from Hodgkin's disease. In fact the value of medicinal products from similar sources is around $40 billion per annum. And if we are losing out collectively, what about the lending agencies? (SEE BOX 3).

From material supplied by Richard Sandbrook, Jim Barns, Bruce Rich and others.

BOX 3

Reform is possible

The World Bank and all the other multilateral and bilateral development agencies are very conscious of their critics on the environment and cultural fronts. In many ways they are caught in a cleft stick. On the one hand the public want to see more done to accelerate development; on the other people criticise the result. Many of the difficulties arise because of the speed at which projects are planned and then carried out.

Recent moves in the United States have brought matters to a head. There is now a major political pressure on the World Bank to put better environmental controls into its project cycle and to invest more in the Third World's capacity to cope. This should mean more research, and having, for environmental purposes, better planning by way of environmental assessments and public consultation and maybe fewer large scale projects.

Environmental protection and development for human needs must be made compatible; there is no alternative to the relief of poverty. The answer, often termed sustainable development, must follow but it is no easy path. Successful development along these lines has been carried out by the voluntary agencies such as Oxfam and the Save the Children Fund over the years but on a limited scale. Governments and the agencies they finance have a vital role to play. They have carried out hunderds of successful schemes — when the needs of people and the limits of nature have been recognised. What is needed is more of the same.

CHAPTER 8

THE KEY TO SURVIVAL

Symbiotic Technologies present industry with its greatest challenge since the information revolution. Though ST, as the sector reports show, represents a whole new range of opportunities in a wide variety of sectors it also can pose a considerable threat to established interests. Where there is a winner enjoying greater gain or success with a Symbiotic Technology there is often a loser left holding a threatened or redundant product or inefficient process.

The risk of obsolescence is always present in commercial life as the size of the business graveyard shows. Advances in technology and changes in markets have always caught out the unprepared, unimaginative and dogmatic. In the 19th century the "Pony Express" was superseded by the telegraph and canal barges by the railways. In their turn in the twentieth century the railways and tram companies have largely given way to the automobile in their countries of origin. The Hollywood giants were swallowed by television and corner stores have been eclipsed by supermarkets. Some companies planned and were able to change with the times; others didn't and have either disappeared or were swallowed by their rivals.

Threat or opportunity?

Symbiotic Technologies directly give the innovator the competitive edge through being more cost effective and through being more attractive to consumers. Indirectly they can grant the innovator an advantage for legislators are presented with the chance of bringing in stricter controls in an environmentally sensitive conventional market on the grounds that a cleaner alternative is now available. As such Symbiotic Technologies represent the major environment linked risk to a company — that of displacement of its conventional products, processes or services by environmentally friendlier methods that appeal to its markets for standard reasons such as lower costs. This risk of ST displacement in some sectors is forming one of the most significant forces for change. Companies are being faced with the choice of adopting new practices within certain environmentally defined parameters or disappearing.

A familiar example is provided by the campaigns to remove lead from petrol which have presented both the oil and motor industries with one of their major challenges to date. Lean burn engines and emission controllers or "catalytic converters", both arguably ST opportunities for some companies, provide possible answers. The suppliers of lead additive though are in an unenviable and precarious position and face the constant threat of displacement if lean burn is ever universally adopted.

Alternative energy supply techniques such as portable windmills for nomads, giant wind turbines for tropical islands, solar power, burning rice husks and other agricultural waste and biogas installations all have the potential to nibble away at the edges of traditional oil markets. This is because they can affect factors like the demand for local diesel generated power. But it is worth remembering, though the oil companies may suffer little or even benefit through being involved in these programmes, what will happen to, say, the diesel generator manufacturers if their markets are eroded in this fashion?

As the chapter on energy conservation pointed out, builders are now expected by some customers to provide more energy efficient buildings than any minimum standards required by law whether they want to or not. In other words market forces are effectively dictating that the interests of those in construction who cannot or will not provide more energy efficient structures will ultimately suffer.

This more efficient use of energy is cutting down on waste, but "Waste" itself presents a wide variety of commercial opportunies as the Waste chapter shows. The chapter also points out that waste issues can

ERODING DIESEL GENERATED POWER MARKETS? FIELD TRIALS OF A
TRANSPORTABLE WIND-POWER SYSTEM DESIGNED FOR NOMADIC USE
IN MONGOLIA.
(Photo: Northumbrian Energy Workshop Ltd.)

result in speeding up of displacement if a process or its by-products are so sensitive or unacceptable that a complete no-compromise ban is anticipated or imposed.

In agriculture agrobiological sprays, biological pest control methods, fluid sowing techniques, electrostatic spraying systems or simply innovative management practices all pose challenges to traditional agrochemical and equipment suppliers and industry, as such a comprehensive term implies, also provides many examples. Besides the implications of lean burn engines there are asbestos-free roofing sheets, water-based (as opposed to organic solvent-based) coach paints, home carbonating kits and new biotechnology-linked developments all replacing or poised to affect the markets of conventional products. As both the industry and waste chapters point out 3M actually had a policy of considering the environmental factor across the board, reducing costs, improving competitiveness and eliminating much pollution in many separate projects.

But who else should consider the green factor?

So commonsense dictates that companies wanting to minimise risks to their existing operations or to explore new opportunities should be considering the green factor, otherwise their interests may suffer through an environmentally conscious rival who has appeared with a better product which displaces their own. However commercial history with its past closures and difficulties shows that what action is necessary or just plain commonsense need not be followed by an industry, particularly if the action appears in some way connected with the bogey "conservation". The spectre of future problems and possible cut-throat competition may seem remote and irrelevant when weighed by some industrial decision makers alongside current commitments and responsibilities. But outside of the organisation there are those with a controlling interest to whom it is of vital importance that companies are considering the green factor at the planning stage: **financiers.**

Businesses need backers in the form of institutions or individuals. Even the institutions such as banks and venture capital funds need investors. If risks to financiers' interests are to be minimised then they should be ensuring that the environmental factor has been accounted for on their investment. Commercial difficulties can affect customers, jobs and managers' careers. They also affect the return on any backers' investment.

BOX 1.

Environment-Linked Risks

These can affect businesses in a surprising variety of ways, sometimes not immediately associated with environmental issues. Can any of the following in what is not an exhaustive list affect your or any other organisation you can think of?

Location Problems — from siting hydro-electric schemes to a simple refusal of planning permission after an expensive initial project study,

Supply Problems — from resource mismanagement and scarcity through to disruptive action by key groups,

Stiffer Legislation — from measures requiring further expenditure to maintain a process to those appearing through lobbying for a less sensitive alternative,

Health and Safety issues — from ensuring safety in production through

unexpected problems with materials supplied to market to discovering a local costly-to-correct hazard not directly connected with an organisation's activities,

Pollution Problems — affecting supplies, location neighbours, production, waste disposal and investment,

Key Groups — from unnecessary action by misinformed staff and consumers through to highly professional lobbying and direct action against a sensitive product or process,

And ultimately:

DISPLACEMENT — being knocked out of a market by a fitter competitor with a Symbiotic Technology.

The chapter on Finance and Development gave some spectacular instances of investments at risk through failure to adequately consider the environmental factor. In the case of the Aswan Dam the repercussions of inadequate impact analyses were felt in a range of sectors and yet arguably the problems like increased incidence of water-based disease, though broadly environmental in origin, could have been pre-empted and the integrity of the project maintained.

Now it's been said the classic financier's retort to those submitting a request for backing in the form of a business plan is "You're the expert". The implication is that if the bottom line or projected return on investment is attractive, particularly if the submission concerns a currently fashionable sector, then the project can expect support. A business plan though is designed to tell potential backers a number of things which, as experience has shown, they need to know when assessing the viability of a proposal. Such factors include the experience of the managerial team, detailed cash flow forecasts and sales estimates. Despite the "You're the expert" rejoinder the plans with patently unrealistic or spurious proposals, say in marketing ("It's so good, everyone will want one once the word gets round") must often be weeded out on the basis of previous knowledge of similar ventures in a given sector.

The question is how many financiers look to see if those submitting proposals have considered the green factor? Almost certainly it is very few outside the major international lending agencies who themselves have a chequered record on green-conscious lending as chapter 7 shows. Yet besides displacement and the consequences of polluting businesses can be affected by a whole range of environment-linked risks (SEE BOX 1) which, as they can range from difficulties in obtaining planning permission through tougher legislation to health and safety issues, are often not recognised as being broadly environmental in origin. But if conscious of the environment-linked risk factor a brief ST analysis looking up the chains of supply and down the proposed routes of sale could help identify sensitive issues and then show whether any pre-emptive measures including insuring where appropriate (SEE BOX 2) had been built into forecasts by the project proposers to avoid future costly remedial action.

If these questions are not asked and if care is not taken over investments financiers could find themselves treading the path to the plots in the commercial graveyard reserved for those organisations falling foul of environmental issues. Indeed it would be an interesting exercise to discover how many financial institutions have experienced difficulties because they have not considered the green factor during lending. And in future just as the construction companies' customers

BOX 2.

Insuring for Corporate and Environmental Protection

— At Seveso, Italy, a safety valve burst in a plant causing an explosion which released a cloud of toxic chemical. Over 1,000 people were evacuated and many received damages. The authorities claimed £270 million for the clean up.

— An oil pipeline joint was loosened by vibrations from a nearby railway line. A leak developed, so slow it was only detected when the oil was discovered in the water table. Clean up costs were £200,000.

— A pig farmer was obliged to pay damages, determined in court, to neighbours inconvenienced by the smell of his farm.

Lots of similar cases show companies in many sectors can incur major extra costs through the accidental affects of their activities on the environment.

One insurance company, ERAS (International) Ltd coined the phrase "Environmental Impairment Liability" and pioneered this type of cover when most insurers were avoiding it because of the apparently endless pitfalls.

They used "environmental impairment" in their policies as not all incidents could be described as pollution, classifying it as:

1. The emission, discharge, dispersal, disposal, seepage, release or escape of any liquid, solid, gaseous or thermal irritant, contaminant or pollutant into or upon land, the atmosphere or any water-course or body of water, and,

2. The generation of smell, noises, vibrations, light, electricity, radiation, changes in temperature or any other sensory phenomena but not fire or explosion.

The policies, though subject to certain geographical and other exclusions, cover such liabilities as bodily injury, death and property damage through a company's activities. They also provide environmental protection in a broader sense, covering interference with amenities protected by law and the costs of cleaning up after an accident.

Taking out the cover gives further environmental protection. Risks are rated from a specially commissioned reference manual which defines the potential claims from the different activities of more than 100 types of industry. Factors affecting the rating (and size of premiums) include waste disposal methods, management attitudes and the standard of "housekeeping". The insurer's survey may reveal undetected risks and cover can be made dependent on meeting statutory standards or improving current practices.

The insurer's audit can also be a useful check on internal safeguards and controls.

expect energy conscious buildings if they are going to buy, investors may expect environment-linked risk conscious institutions if they are going to invest.

There is another advantage to financiers of looking to see if business proposals consider the environmental factor: it can help identify those with a greater potential for success because they are demonstrating thoroughness, a prerequisite of good managerial practice. A company with a sound energy or waste management policy devised and initiated at the outset is one which is demonstrably going to take care of its resources and costs so the maximum possible can be contributed to revenue generating activities in development, production and sales. It is also a company that can be expected to compete on equitable terms with another in the sector concerned that is similarly cost-conscious.

Yet financiers and management can only be thorough if the correct information is available. But already there are excellent sources of information on environmental issues ranging from the publications of various interest groups through general literature to informative magazines like the monthly ENDS report which are aimed at the busy general manager. If the information is not available then there are tried and tested techniques like Environmental Impact Analysis that can help derive it, consultancies and training programmes.

The possiblility of tougher environment-linked legislation appearing in a market is one risk that should be continually assessed way past the project setup stage. This could affect costs and even the viability of the product or the organisations. Though Chapter 2 pointed out this requires some initiative on the part of legislators nonetheless the risk still persists and could increase as politicians slowly awake to environmental concern because they perceive its "green vote" potential.

How genuine this political concern is arguable if it is only expressed to "buy" green votes. However it does exist and will continue to grow. It is inevitable then that some political decision makers will eventually recognise the significance and potential of Symbiotic Technologies. But ST is not a doma; it is simply a category of human activity that is advantageous for all to explore. As such it is apolitical. Certainly it can be argued that politics are only relevant to ST in certain circumstances such as ST innovators lobbying for legislation that hits the environmentally unacceptable technologies of the competition.

Though many environmental problems require political will to resolve them this is often because they were created through political factors in the first place. But despite the scramble for the green vote, the environment should not be a political football. ST certainly isn't for whether it appears in a free market or centrally planned ecomomy it will still be worth exploring or encouraging by political decision makers due to its inherent advantages. Indeed as it will probably appear anyway the only party political advantage to be wrested from the situation is in creating circumstances that further favour its growth. Measures could include tax concessions on wind farms or fuelwood plantations or, more directly, there could be governmental environmental agencies researching, identifying and promoting ST opportunities. Any opportunities that could help ease the administration of the horns of possible conserve or develop dilemmas would be of particular interest.

The spin off benefits then accruing to those political decision makers encouraging ST would be similar to those envisaged by any in government trying to stimulate the economy and would include, say, seeing improved job opportunites, new sources of commercial tax revenue or goods for export. Being perceived as environmentally conscious would come as a bonus if the political decision maker wanted to draw their supporters' attention to the side effects of their encouraging ST.

The Key

Symbiotic Technology though is not a magic solution to global environmental ills and it is overly simplistic to think of ST as some all-powerful panacea. But to some decision makers it represents a very powerful environmental problem-solving tool as commercial attempts to develop cleaner technologies and the environmental lobby's encouragement of these testify. Some man made environmental problems are to a certain extent managerial problems, if a managing agency can be identified as having overall responsibility in a given situation. The solutions often lie in practical managerial packages that take account of the real world of endless compromise in which commerce and politicians have to live.

Managerial packages that take account of ecological factors have already provided the answers to many problems, as in a classic case of nearly forty years ago from the cotton growing area of the Cañete valley in Peru. Initially, introducing DDT and two other organochlorine pesticides in 1949 was highly successful as yields rose from 494 kg per hectare in 1950 to 728 kg in 1954. The 1955/56 season though was a disaster. Pests were now resistant to the chemicals despite increases in the frequency of application and a switch to organophosphate sprays. These and animals promoted to pest status through their controlling predators being wiped out took their toll. Yields dropped to 332 kg per hectare.

The solution to the problem lay in improved managerial practices. Pesticide and marginal land use were strictly controlled, cultivation methods altered to discriminate against the life cycles of pests and insect predators were reintroduced from neighbouring valleys which, fortunately, had not been sprayed. Cotton yields rose to 526 kg per hectare a year after these measures were taken and since yields, and therefore returns, have reached their highest ever levels.

Cañete is far from unique and more recently V R Philips of the U.K. National Institute of Agricultural Engineering looked at engineering solutions to the problems caused by agriculture and concluded, "In five years time, new technology will have 'designed out' the need for much of the management care presently necessary". The management care he cited as able to reduce the environmental impact of agriculture on freshwater runoff included mathematical modelling for better-timed and lower nitrate fertiliser application and careful monitoring of slurry spreading rates. Amongst other possible technological solutions he claims will supersede the need for some managerial care are developing self sufficient crops that can fix their own nitrogen, like peas and beans can due to the nitrogen-fixing bacteria in their root systems, and solids separation, composting and anaerobic digestion for dealing with slurry.

In each case what is effectively ST analysis (unnamed) is revealing both the problem and the solutions and the remedial action, applied or recommended, contains a battery of Symbiotic Technologies from improved crop management to biological pest control. In solving other environmental problems these managerial packages have been, are and will continue to be founded on Symbiotic Technologies and the principles of ST analysis (SEE BOX 3).

Going beyond problem-solving it is well known that the best, if sometimes seemingly hypothetical, way of dealing with problems is to anticipate them and where possible take preventative measures. This book has consistently argued that failing to consider the environment at the planning state can lead to unnecessary difficulties and, in the case of commerce, potential losses. Identifying Symbiotic Technologies, exploiting the opportunities they offer and undertaking ST analyses means the environmental factor is practically being considered as part of the planning process.

By its very nature, named or not, Symbiotic Technology lies at the heart of plans for any sustainable development or conservation and development programme. Arguably decision makers could expect greater chances of acceptance of plans and increased chances of a successful project through reduced environment-linked risks by building ST into their proposals for development packages.

BOX 3.

Symbiotic Technology? — That Depends . . .

Waterbased coachpaints have been developed by ICI. In their own right they possess distinct ST characteristics as they contain far less organic solvents than conventional coach paints and so they are a welcome innovation, contributing to improved working conditions and reduced atmospheric pollution through lower solvent emissions. They are also welcome from an investment point of view as a system using Aquabased paints cost much less to install than a conventional system.

To judge if an innovation is truly a Symbiotic Technology though means seeing it **in context.** For instance such a system would be a wise choice as part of an engineering development package from the point of view of cost and local environmental protection. But what if the new factory were to produce bulldozers to log out the receiving county's rainforests?

Rainforests can be the losers in a number of ST-at-first-glance scenarios. A proportion of alcohol in petroleum (gasoline) produces "gasohol" for vehicles but what if forests have been indiscriminately cleared for sugarcane plantations to produce the sugar for fermentation to alcohol? Naturally occurring insecticides like **Pyrethrum** are attractive but again land has to be cleared to grow it.

Looking beyond the boundaries of the particular enterprise or project, performing an **ST analysis,** is vital to whether a particular product, process or package can be judged a Symbiotic Technology.

The prime reason for the analysis though is **self-interest.** It is the main method of identifying any environment-linked risks to a project so helping anticipate and avoid possible problems, difficulties and commercial losses.

Symbiotic Technology can be expected to spread globally through self interest, promoted because of the multilateral gains it offers to different interested parties in commerce, markets, government and the environmental lobby. It will form the basis of prosperity in many business sectors as it is adopted by go-ahead success-orientated organisations. The traditional and the conservative will go down the well trodden path of obsolescence to obscurity. If considering the green factor is now a prerequisite for commercial survival then researching and developing Symbiotic Technologies is the realistic way it can be accounted for in those plans. Commercially, ST provides a signpost to success or at least to increased security. And globally, Symbiotic Technology has even greater significance: it is the key to our future survival . . .

REFERENCES AND FURTHER READING

The specific references in the industry chapter were:

1. World Industry Conference on Environmental Management (WICEM): Outcome and reactions, Peter Bunyard and John Elkington, **Industry and Environment** Special Issue No. 5, UNEP Industry and Environment Office, Paris, 1985.
2. **The World Conservation Strategy**, UNEP/IUCN/WWF 1980.
3. **The Conservation and Development Programme for the U.K.**, Kogan Page Ltd., London, 1983.
4. **Improving Environment Co-operation: The roles of Multinational Corporations and Developing Countries,** World Resources Institute, Washington, D.C. 1984.
5. Bayer AG: Buying Time for Cleaner Technologies, **ENDS Report 82**, Environmental Data Services Ltd., London, November 1981, pp 9-11.
6. **Sustainable Development in an Industrial Economy**, CEED Conference, Cambridge, U.K. 24-25 June 1985.
7. **The Environmental Implications and Applications of Biotechnology,** John Elkington and Jonathan Shopley, CEED Discussion Paper 2, The U.K. Centre for Economic and Environmental Development, 1985.

The remainder of the book has not given reference sources for many of the ideas it contains. However readers wanting to follow up some of these ideas could look to the following:

For an easy-to-grasp summary of global environmental problems see Norman Myers' edited volume entitled *The Gaia Atlas of Planet Management* (Pan Books, 1985). Robert Allen's *How to save the World* (Kogan Page, 1980), and *Ecology for Beginners* by Croall and Rankin (Pantheon, 1980) are also good guides to the basics. For the specialist Wagstaffe's *The Evolution of Middle Eastern Landscapes* (Croom Helm, 1985) gives some insights into the environmental impact of ancient activities.

On technology and development the pace was set by E. F. Schumacher's *Small is Beautiful* (Blond & Briggs 1973). The *Careless Technology* edited by Farvar and Milton (Tom Stacey 1973) gives many case studies of environmental problems affecting development and *Building a Sustainable Society* (Norton, 1981) is Lester R. Brown's perspective on why and how an environmentally friendlier approach to development should be adopted. The excellent *ENDS Report* is published monthly by Environmental Data Services Ltd. and is required reading for anyone serious about developing an environmental policy or simply monitoring the impact of their organisation's activities. The *Pollution Abatement Technology Award* booklets published by the Royal Society of Arts give details of products and processes that reduce environmental impact.

Further reading on agriculture in the U.K. include the Royal Commission's Seventh Report on pollution, *Agriculture and Pollution* (Cmnd 7644, HMSO, 1979) and *Conservation in Perspective*, edited by Andrew Warren and Brian Goldsmith (Wiley, Chicester, 1983) provides an excellent and comprehensive account of ecological management of all the key habitat types. The general debate over agriculture and the countryside is covered in Philip Lowe, Graham Cox, Malcolm MacEwan, Timothy O'Riordan and Michael Winter's, *Countryside Conflicts: The Politics of Farming, Forestry and Conservation* (Gower/Maurice Temple Smith, London, 1985). The Nature Conservancy Council report is entitled *Nature Conservation in Great Britain* (Northminster House,

Peterborough, 1984), while the
Countryside Commission study on *A Better
Future for the Uplands* (CCP 162,
Cheltenham, 1984) is an excellent review
of the social, economic and environmental
problems affecting the uplands. More
generally the Commonwealth Agriculture
Bureaux produce a booklet on their
Biological Control Service called *25 years of
achievement*.

It is customary to include a list of
useful names and addresses but really for
the U.K. the best comprehensive source is
the *Directory of British Associations* published
by C B D Research, though the
Conservation Review, published annually by
the Conservation Foundation, lists both
useful addresses and interesting
conservation and development projects.

THE WRITERS

JOHN ELKINGTON
(INDUSTRY)

John Elkington is a futurist and a
leading writer on the revolutionary
changes taking place in the World's
industries. He has acted as consultant to
many national and international
organisations and as a Director of
Earthlife U.K. Ltd. is working on a
number of sustainable development
projects. His books number among them
*The Ecology of Tomorrow's World, Pollution
1990, Sun Traps: The Renewable Energy
Forecast* and *The Poisoned Womb*. He is an
assessor of the U.K. Pollution Abatement
Technology Awards and is currently
preparing a report for the Nature
Conservancy Council on guidelines for
onshore oil development.

MAREK MAYER
(WASTE)

Marek 'Mayer is Editor of the ENDS
Report, a monthly journal published by
Environmental Data Services Ltd. which
briefs industry on the environmental
pressures which could affect its business
prospects and publicises examples of
sound environmental practice in industry.
Environmental Data Services has carried
out consultancy work for the Department
of the Environment, and provides
intelligence and publicity services for
clients engaged in manufacturing and
waste management.

TIMOTHY O'RIORDAN
(AGRIGULTURE AND ENVIRONMENTAL HEALTH)

Timothy O'Riordan is Professor of
Environmental Sciences at the University
of East Anglia. He has taught in Canada,
New Zealand and the United States and
has made a special study of
environmentalism as a philosophy and
practical concept. He is Chairman of the
Strategy Committee of the Broads
Authority and a member of the Advisory
Committee for England of the Nature
Conservancy Council. He is also
Chairman of the Environmental Initiatives
Programme of the Economic and Social
Research Council.

STEVE ROBINSON
(EDITOR)

Steve Robinson qualified in Zoology,
Management Studies and Fisheries
Management before working in Aid in
Malawi as a Fisheries Officer. On
returning to the U.K. he joined a small
engineering business and contrasted this
commercial experience with the aid work
and contemporary opinions on
environmental issues. Deciding that
decision makers needed to know more
about what emerging techniques were to
their advantage, he developed the idea of
naming Symbiotic Technology after
talking to a wide variety of people in
industry, commerce, consultancy and
conservation. He is currently employed in
general management at the
Commonwealth Institute which presented
the opportunity to follow through this
project and is a committee member of the
Business Graduates Association.

RICHARD SANDBROOK
(FINANCE AND DEVELOPMENT)

Richard Sandbrook is Vice President
for Policy at the International Institute of
Environment and Development (IIED)
and is a member of their Environment
Liaison Board. He is also Company
Secretary of Earth Resources Research Ltd
(ERR). Qualified in marine and terrestrial
ecology he has worked previously in
consultancy for Arthur Anderson & Co.
and as Administrative Director for Friends
of the Earth U.K. (FoE) He is editor of a
number of FoE and ERR publications and
has written a number of papers, features
and articles on North/South relations, with
particular emphasis on the environment,
and has appeared on television and radio

on environmental and development
matters. He is married with two children.

ANDREW WARREN
(ENERGY CONSERVATION)

Andrew Warren is the Director of the
Association for the Conservation of Energy
(ACE). Born in 1948, he was educated at
Rugby School and the University of
Exeter. Upon graduation, he worked in
advertising for Saatchi & Saatchi
Garland-Compton Limited, before
becoming secretary to the Movement for
London campaign. Upon the foundation of
ACE in 1981, he was appointed its first
Director. He was the co-author of the TV
series "Fancy Saying a Thing Like That".
He is an underwriter at Lloyds. He is
married to a solicitor, has two sons and
lives in Essex.

THANKS

This project would not have been possible without the generous support of the sponsors, The Environment Foundation and the cooperation of the promoters, the Conservation Foundation and the Commonwealth Institute.

Besides these organisations many individuals need my personal thanks for their help in getting the project to this stage including, of course, the sector writers and especially David Bellamy, James Porter, Director of the Commonwealth Institute and David Shreeve of the Conservation Foundation.

I'm also grateful to:

Peter Brown, Tarporley Travel; Tom Burke, The Green Alliance; Tom Cairns, CoEnCo; Chris Crossley and the National Westminster Bank; Dr. John Davoll, The Conservation Society; Ed Dawson, CoEnCo; Martyn Dunleavy, The Commonwealth Institute; Jane Dunmore, Clean Air magazine; Henry Durowse, Shell U.K. Ltd; Drs. Bob & Judy Foster Smith; Alan Greenwood; Ros Kidman Cox, BBC Wildlife Magazine; Peter Kukla; Miranda McKearney, Commonwealth Institute; Peter Manley, Durham University Business School; George Medley, World Wildlife Fund U.K.; Nick Newbery, Commonwealth Institute; Mike Pullin, Commonwealth Institute; Annie Ritson; Stacey Shapiro; Gaynor Shutte, BBC Radio; Anne Tennant, BBC Radio; Dr. Ted Thairs, CBI; Robert Troake, BP International Environmental Control Centre; Dr. P. Wagstaffe, Southampton University; Charlotte Whitaker, Conservation Foundation.

Thanks for the photographs and other material reproduced here go to:
H. P. Bulmer Ltd.; The Electricity Council; Emstar Ltd.; Environmental Data Services Ltd.; Eras (International) Ltd.; Greenpeace; ICI Paints Division; ICI Plant Protection Division; London Regional Transport; Microbial Resources Ltd.; Northumbrian Energy Workshop Ltd.

This is far from a complete list though I hope no one will take offence at any unintentional omissions.

THE SPONSORS

The Environment Foundation, Ibex House, Minories, London EC3N 1HJ. Telephone: 01 709 0744

The Environment Foundation is a charitable Trust with the object of promoting environmental protection. It is funded by the Lloyds-based Clarkson Puckle Group of international insurance and reinsurance brokers. In the 1970's, after considerable study of the insurance aspects of pollution the Group set up a completely new type of world-wide insurance to protect industrial companies against the liabilities which might arise from non-accidental, long term pollution and damage to the environment. As they felt they should make a positive contribution to improving the environment, a fixed percentage of this **Environmental Impairment Liability** was set aside for a fund for risk improvement — hence the Environment Foundation. Initially known as the ERAS Foundation (for Environmental Risk Analysis System) the Environment Foundation has also been a key sponsor of the highly successful U.K. Pollution Abatement Technology Awards (PATAS).

THE PROMOTERS

The Conservation Foundation, 11a West Halkin Street, London SW1 8JL. Telephone: 01 235 1743

The Conservation Foundation was launched in 1982. One of its aims is to provide an "umbrella" for conservation groups and individuals involved in constructive conservation. It has no members and does not itself get involved in practical conservation work. Instead, it aims to help and publicise the efforts of those who do and when requested seek sponsorship for them. The Foundation covers all aspects of Conservation from Buildings to Butterflies including engineering and development. Amongst the companies actively involved is the Ford Motor Company which has sponsored the Conservation Awards for four years in programmes now running in seven European countries. The Foundation gives away £250,000 annually but is constantly looking at ways to produce additional funds for the many demands made on it and hopes that its involvement with this book will produce further finance to extend its work.

The Commonwealth Institute, Kensington High Street, London W8 6NQ. Telephone: 01 603 4535

The Commonwealth Institute is Britain's symbol of commitment to the people of the 49 countries making up the Commonwealth. The dazzling cultural and geographical diversity of the Commonwealth is explored through a kaleidoscope of in- and out-door performing and visual arts events, exhibitions in its custom-built Galleries and through conferences, seminars and workshops on contemporary issues. It is a centre for key International and diplomatic functions as well as a long-remembered and popular classroom, for schools are made especially welcome. There is a Library and Information service, a restaurant with a distinctly Commonwealth menu, a bookshop and a Friends Organisation for visitors wanting to become more closely involved.